MW00713418

ON YOUR OWN

Scrumptious, fail-safe recipes and kitchen advice

Alice Stern

Straight Arrow Press

Cover Design: Irene Imfeld Graphic Design
Graphic Assistance: Kandy Petersen
Advisor: Jack Howell, Morning Sun Press

Straight Arrow Press
639 Glorietta Blvd.
Lafayette, CA 94549
Phone: 510-283-3205
Fax: 510-283-5703

In memory of Aunt Rebie

ACKNOWLEDGMENTS

It is with deep appreciation that I'd like to like to thank the following special people for their help with this project:

Gary Stern, my husband of 30 years, for many long hours of computer assistance and for unflagging support and encouragement; Todd Stern and Andrea Stern, my children, for computer instruction and recipe refinements; Laura Niebling, for the many, many hours of tedious and patient editing, for constant support, and for the wonderful Pasta Puttanesca and Chocolate Chip Oatmeal Cookie recipes. I am truly blessed to have such a devoted friend; Trudy Stern, Charlotte Waggoner, Alice Breakstone, Jennifer Breakstone, Debbie Goldberg, Trudy McMahon, Gayle Goldman, Benji Kushins, Julia Quarry; for recipes and/or kitchen testing; Kandy Petersen, for graphic assistance; and, to Jack Howell of Morning Sun Press, for his help, advice and assistance in taking my manuscript and turning it in to a book.

CONTENTS

Baguette Pizza   45
Pesto Pizza   46
Spinach Balls with Yogurt Dip   47
Garlic and Onion Bread Strips   48
Best Ever Cornbread   49
Black Bean and Corn Quesadillas   50

SOUPS
Shrimp, Rice and Broccoli Chowder   52
Chicken Curry Soup   53
Chinese Vegetable Soup   54
Hearty Split Pea Soup   55
Lentil Chard Soup   56
Carrot Chutney Soup   57
Broccoli Apple Soup   58
Mushroom and Potato Soup   59
Tucson Corn Chowder   61
Mexican Vegetable Soup   62
Lentil Vegetable Soup   64

SALAD DRESSINGS AND SALADS

Salad Dressings
Basic Vinaigrette   66
Honey Mustard Vinaigrette   66
Creamy Herb Salad Dressing   67
Bleu Cheese Salad Dressing   68

Salads
New Caesar Salad   70
Southwest Chicken Salad   72
Curry Yogurt Chicken Salad   73
Ginger Rice Salad   74
Corn Salad   76
French Potato Salad   77
Coleslaw, Deli-Style   78
Red Cabbage Coleslaw   79

PASTA

MEAT

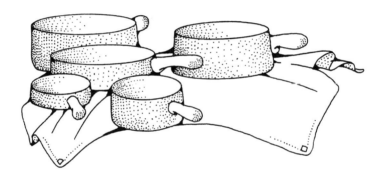

INTRODUCTION

This book was written for young adults who have added cooking to their daily "To Do" list, and who enjoy good food.

The introduction of a book is often ignored, but I hope that you will continue reading now that you have started. I'd like to take this opportunity to share with you my enthusiasm about cooking and creating delicious snacks and meals for yourself, for family and for friends.

I honestly can't understand what people mean when they say, "I can't cook", because I have always felt that if you can read, you can cook. This theory, so to speak, was further refined by my son who claims that if you have taken chemistry lab even at the high school level, and have been given a set of detailed set of instructions to follow, you can be a good cook.

My children have enjoyed cooking as youngsters and have evolved into very creative cooks when they left for college and beyond. As their Mom, I decided to record our favorite recipes for them and to include some hints and time saving measures I've learned over the years I've been cooking. This family project grew and developed a life of its own, and I spent many enjoyable hours at the computer (slowly learning as I went along - now that was a real challenge!). During this infant phase of the project, I was asked by friends, neighbors and cooking students if I would share my efforts.

I hope you like what I have compiled. The great majority of my recipes have much of the fat reduced with regard to today's concern for a healthy diet. The other recipes, those with a fair amount of fat, are also part of our life, yet to be enjoyed occasionally. However, the main criterion for being included in this collection, beyond relative ease of preparation, is taste: every recipe was chosen from among the hundreds that I have because it is truly delicious and numerous people have enjoyed it. Since I am the only person I know who likes liver, I have not included that recipe. I hope you find this book useful and that you enjoy the time you spend cooking.

If you like being in the kitchen, or wish that you did, take cooking classes. You'll learn from the instructor, and also from your classmates.

Ask your friends and neighbors for help. Invite friends over to share what you have created. Bring food to sick friends (they'll do it for you when you are the sick one). Impress your parents. The more you cook, the more you will learn, and the happier you'll be in the kitchen.

And, be sure to read through the entire recipe before you begin to cook. I always begin my cooking classes with some basic information; becoming familiar with the recipe is one of the points I emphasize. It's no fun to have to drive to the store in the middle of cooking or hope that a neighbor will be able to come to your aid.

In one fall class a young woman smiled knowingly through this discussion. She then shared her recipe for a 24 egg chocolate mousse. "Twenty-four eggs !", we all exclaimed. "This must certainly be the richest mousse ever, or perhaps served a small army." She told us that the recipe instructed to put 12 egg yolks in a large bowl. So she cracked the eggs, and threw the whites into the sink. The next step was to beat the whites until they formed soft peaks. Since they were now down the drain, she went back to the grocery store, promising not to make this kind of mistake again.

Let this book be your guide, but make changes as you see fit. If you don't like olives, and they aren't the main ingredient, eliminate them. It's usually fine to use different herbs and different vinegars, or to reduce the amount of seasonings. Let these recipes be your inspiration to create something new. But most of all, have fun !

GETTING STARTED

SETTING UP YOUR KITCHEN

Below is a basic list of equipment that you might like to consult as you shop. Not all equipment needs to be new. I have found many perfect items at thrift shops and garage sales. Keep in mind that several items have multiple uses: a 9 inch square pan can be used to bake brownies or cook a meatloaf. Also, it isn't necessary, or even a good idea, to have a complete set of any one brand of cookware. Often boxed sets have a pan or two that isn't especially useful. Choose the size and style of pots and pans to suit your needs.

Stove Top:
Saucepans: 1 quart, 3 quart, 6 quart (important size for making soup and cooking pasta)
Steamer insert or collapsible steamer
Wok: for stir-fry dishes
Frying pans: 7 inch, 10 inch, 12 inch (good size to have when preparing for a dinner party) - non-stick finish is great

Oven:
Dutch Oven: for pot roasts and stews
Roasting pan: metal, with removable rack
9 inch square pan
9x13 pan
11x17 pan, also known as a jelly-roll pan
Baking sheet, also called cookie sheet, (2)
Loaf pan (2)
Muffin tin: non-stick finish is best

Knives:

Inexpensive knives aren't any bargain. They become dull quickly and need to be replaced. Buy the best quality knife you can and consider it a life-long investment.

2 paring knives, a 3½ inch and a 4½ inch: for cutting small things
1 medium blade chef's knife: for chopping
1 boning knife: for cutting raw chicken, meat and fish
1 long slicing knife: for slicing roasts, turkey, etc.
1 serrated knife: for slicing bread
1 sharpening steel

For Food Preparation:

Plastic cutting board
Mixing bowls: small, medium and large - can also be used as salad or fruit bowls
Metal or plastic colander: for draining pasta, rinsing fruits and vegetables
Measuring spoons
Measuring cups
Large cooking spoons: be sure to have at least one that is slotted
Wooden spoons
Spatulas: plastic- for combining ingredients and scraping bowls
metal- for turning things and serving
Soup ladle
Vegetable peeler
Garlic press
Hand grater: for shredding cheese, grating carrots, apples, ginger and other vegetables
Wire whisk: for beating eggs, combining liquids
Kitchen timer: **very important-** don't try to guess or try to remember when things are done.

Small appliances:
Toaster or toaster oven
Food processor or mini food processor
Mixer
Blender or hand mixer

When no other tool can do the job:
Can opener
Corkscrew
Salad spinner: for washing and drying greens
Kitchen scale: one that weighs ingredients up to four pounds
Citrus juicer
Citrus zester: for removing the zest, or rind, of lemons and
  limes
Melon baller: obviously for making melon balls, but also for
  easily removing the flesh of soft fruits and vegetables
Cake rack: for cooling cakes and cookies
Cake tester
Pastry blender
Pot holders, kitchen towels

SETTING UP YOUR PANTRY

If space permits, it's nice to have some basics on hand. Remember to read labels and be sure to refrigerate opened items as suggested on the label.

In the Refrigerator:
Milk, low fat or non-fat
Unflavored yogurt
Butter, unsalted
Eggs
Juice
Parmesan cheese, freshly grated
Salad ingredients - lettuce, ripe tomatoes, cucumber, carrots, celery
Fresh fruit - apples, oranges, lemons, seasonal fruits
Fresh ginger
Fresh parsley
Dijon mustard
Horseradish
Mayonnaise
Ketchup

In the freezer:
Frozen chopped spinach
Frozen chopped broccoli
Frozen corn
Frozen peas and carrots

In a cool place:
Potatoes, russet and red skinned
Onions
Garlic
White wine, red wine and sherry for cooking - buy what you would like to drink, and not something marked "cooking wine"

On the shelf:

Chicken stock, canned
Beef bouillon cubes
Canned chopped tomatoes
Tomato sauce
Tomato paste
Tomato puree
Cream style corn
Canned beans: pinto, kidney, garbanzo
Black olives - whole and sliced
Marinated artichoke hearts
Canned green chilies
Capers
Pasta, dried
White rice, brown rice
Lentils, split peas, barley
Flour
White sugar, brown sugar
Honey
Baking powder, baking soda
Chocolate chips
Cornmeal
Wheat germ
Bran cereal, breakfast cereal
Cornstarch
Vegetable spray
Raisins
Maple syrup
Vegetable oil
Olive oil
Sesame oil
Soy sauce
Breadcrumbs

Seasonings:

Salt

Whole black peppercorns (and a grinder)

Cayenne pepper

Red pepper flakes

Garlic salt

Vinegar - red wine, white wine, cider, Balsamic

Dried herbs- basil, oregano, thyme, bay leaf, rosemary, dill

Spices - ground cinnamon, ground allspice, ground cloves, ground ginger, ground nutmeg, ground cumin, curry powder, chili powder, paprika, turmeric

Worcestershire sauce

Tabasco

Vanilla extract

HOW TO...

QUICK AND EASY HINTS FOR PERFORMING ROUTINE TASKS

HOW TO COOK CHICKEN for chicken salad or other dishes requiring cooked chicken, the easy way...

Always wash chicken in cold water before cooking. You can use chicken with or without the skin and bones. Place chicken breasts in a large saucepan and cover with lots of cold water - at least 3 inches over the top of the chicken. Bring to a boil, cover and remove the pot from the heat. Using tongs or a large fork, take the chicken out of the water after 20 minutes. Cut into one piece to see that it is cooked through. If it isn't, return the chicken to the pot, bring the same water to a boil, cover, remove from the heat and let sit for another 20 minutes. Cool slightly before handling.

HOW TO COOK WHITE RICE, the easy way...

In a small saucepan combine 1 cup rice with 1½ cups cold water. Bring to a boil over high heat, reduce heat to the lowest setting, cover and cook for 10 minutes. One cup of raw rice yields 2½ cups cooked rice.

HOW TO COOK POTATOES for potato salad or to serve as a side dish...

The best way to cook potatoes for potato salad is not to boil them as is most often done, but rather to steam them. Cooked this way the potatoes are never heavy with excess water. Place the scrubbed or peeled sliced potatoes in a steamer over boiling water. A collapsible steamer also works fine. Reduce heat to moderate and cook until the potatoes are tender, about 20 minutes. Remove from the heat and turn into a bowl. If serving as a side dish, sprinkle with chopped parsley.

HOW TO COOK PASTA...

Bring a large pot of water to a boil. Pasta should cook in lots of water. Add 2 teaspoons of oil per pound of pasta to the water (not necessary to measure) to prevent the pasta from sticking to itself. Drop the pasta into the water by handfuls so that the water doesn't stop boiling. Reduce heat a bit and continue cooking until just tender, stirring occasionally. Drain immediately.

HOW TO WASH SPINACH...

Fill a large bowl with cold water. Remove the stems of the spinach, immerse in the water and agitate slightly. When the water becomes dirty, remove the spinach and set aside, drain the water and fill the bowl again with cold water. (Be sure to remove the spinach and set aside rather than pouring the dirty water out of the bowl over the almost clean spinach!) Add the spinach and toss again. Do this until the water in the bowl is left clean when the spinach is added and tossed. Remove the spinach and dry in a salad spinner or on a towel.

HOW TO WASH MUSHROOMS...

If the mushrooms aren't very dirty, they can be wiped off with a damp paper towel. If they are dirty, fill a large bowl with cold water and place mushrooms in the water. Agitate slightly, and using your fingers as sifters, lift the mushrooms out of the water, leaving the residue behind. Immediately dry with a paper towel. The mushrooms should be in the water briefly so they don't absorb too much water. When you buy mushrooms, place them in a paper bag and put that into a plastic bag. Store in the refrigerator. The paper bag will absorb the refrigerator moisture that is harmful to the mushrooms. Mushrooms can be kept about three days before they begin to turn. Wash just before using.

HOW TO WASH LEEKS...

Cut off the tough dark green end, usually the last several inches, and the roots. Slice the leek down the center and wash each section. Take care to wash between the layers since dirt tends to accumulate there while growing.

HOW TO WASH ASPARAGUS...

Wash the asparagus under cold water, being careful not to break or bruise the tip. Hold the asparagus stalk in both hands and break off at the spot where the woody tip meets the edible part of the stalk. This end will just snap off. Don't place ends in the garbage disposal - these ends, as well as artichoke leaves, tend to jam the disposal.

HOW TO WASH SALAD GREENS...

Wash salad greens in cold water and dry. To wash iceberg lettuce, cut out the core and hold the head under running water. Gently separate the leaves to allow water to run between them. To wash romaine, leaf lettuce and butter lettuce, cut at the core and hold individual leaves under running water. A salad spinner is the perfect tool for drying the lettuce. Alternatively, shake off the excess water and lay on either a paper towel or a clean kitchen towel. Place the washed greens in either a sealed plastic bag or a plastic container with a lid and refrigerate until needed.

HOW TO PEEL AND SEED TOMATOES...

Often recipes call for peeled tomatoes. Bring a pot of water to a boil, cut out the tomato core and immerse in the water for about 30 seconds, or until the skin begins to loosen. Plunge into a bowl of ice water to stop the cooking. Using a paring knife, gently pull off the skin. It should easily slip off, but if it doesn't, put the tomato back into the boiling water for 15 seconds more.

To seed the tomato, cut it in half, and, holding over the sink or a small bowl, squeeze gently. (Wear an apron because the seeds do spurt). The tomato will release its seeds and some of the pulp. Don't worry that the tomato begins to loose its shape; the next step is to cut it up.

HOW TO GRATE AND STORE GINGER...

Fresh ginger is readily available in the produce section of the grocery store. Buy a piece that feels firm and isn't wrinkled. Break off a knob and peel carefully with a sharp paring knife. Grate using a hand grater or mince with a knife. Store remaining ginger in a sealed plastic bag in the refrigerator. Ginger stays fresh for several weeks. If a part becomes moldy, cut off that moldy section and discard.

HOW TO PEEL AND STORE GARLIC...

A whole bulb of garlic is called a head; an individual section a clove. Buy heads of garlic that feel firm and store them in a cool place. Don't refrigerate garlic. Remove individual cloves as needed. To peel, place on a cutting board and press down with the heel of your hand - the papery covering will splinter. Remove this covering and cut off the dark tip with a small paring knife.

HOW TO HANDLE CHILI PEPPERS...

Cut off the stem and slice chili pepper in half lengthwise. Using a small spoon, carefully remove the seeds, taking care not to get the seeds on your hands. The smaller varieties have the hotter seeds. If you are handling a large quantity of chili peppers, you might consider wearing plastic gloves. Wash hands, cutting board and knife thoroughly before continuing. and be sure not to touch your eyes while you are working with chilies.

HOW TO REMOVE THE ZEST OF CITRUS FRUIT...

Zest is the colored part of the skin of a citrus fruit. It has a lot of flavor and natural oil and is often added to a dish to enhance the citrus flavor. Using a zester, a tool made especially for this purpose, carefully strip the skin, leaving behind the bitter white part. If you don't have a zester, use either a sharp paring knife or a hand grater.

HOW TO BLANCH VEGETABLES...

Bring a large pot of water to a boil. Have nearby a large bowl of ice water. Drop washed and sliced vegetables, or whole fruit, into the boiling water. Leave just until the vegetables change color, about 15 seconds, or the skin on the whole fruit begins to loosen, about 30-45 seconds. Then, with a slotted spoon, remove from the boiling water and place in the ice water to cool.

If different vegetables are being blanched, perhaps for a vegetable tray to be served with dip, do each vegetable separately and start with the lightest color vegetable. Those vegetables to be blanched are carrots, broccoli, cauliflower and green beans. Snow peas are immersed in the boiling water for just for a second or two before being removed.

HOW TO TOAST NUTS...

Preheat oven to 350 degrees. Place shelled nuts on a baking sheet and bake for 5-10 minutes until fragrant, depending on the size of the nuts. Sliced almonds will take about 7 minutes, walnut halves about 10 minutes. Check frequently to prevent over-toasting. Place the hot baked nut meats in a kitchen towel and rub them together to remove the brown skin.

HOW TO MAKE CREME FRAICHE...

In a small jar combine 5 parts cream and 1 part buttermilk. Cover the jar with plastic wrap and wrap in a towel. Leave on the kitchen counter until thickened, usually 24 hours. Room temperature needs to be about 70 degrees. Store in the refrigerator until needed.

HOW TO STORE CHEESE...

Wrap cheese in plastic wrap and always use a new piece of plastic after cutting off some cheese . Keep cheese refrigerated. If mold grows, cut off that part and discard.

HOW TO USE STALE FRENCH BREAD...

When bread becomes too hard to eat, either
(a) re-crisp bread: lightly dampen the bread by running under cold water and place in a 350 degree oven until crisp, about 10 minutes. This works best with bread not more than 2 days old.
(b) make bread crumbs: make sure the bread is completely dried out. Cut into chunks and make bread crumbs in the food processor. Store in the freezer in a sealed plastic bag.
(c) make croutons: slice bread into cubes. Heat a small amount of olive oil in a frying pan over medium heat and brown the bread cubes on all sides. Remove from the heat and sprinkle with garlic salt, if desired.

HOW TO CLEAN SHRIMP...

Peel off the shell, and with a sharp knife make a small cut down the back of the shrimp and remove the vein. Wash well under cold, running water.

COOKING TERMS

Below are some culinary terms to become familiar with. Don't let the length of this list frighten you! You have probably been doing most of these things already without giving the process a name.

Bake - a method of cooking using the dry heat process.
Barbecue - to cook over an open fire which is usually made from briquets or wood.
Baste - to brush with a liquid while cooking to keep the food from drying out.
Batter - the result of combining flour, egg and liquid.
Blanch - to place in boiling water, usually for a very short time.
Blend - to combine two or more ingredients and mix well.
Boil - to heat a liquid until it reaches 212 degrees at sea level. When boiling, splashing bubbles appear on the surface.
Broil - a method of cooking using the dry heat process. When broiling, the heat source is from above, as to broil in an oven.
Broth - the by-product of cooking meat, chicken and/or vegetables in liquid.
Brown - to seal in the juices and give a good color to meat, chicken or fish. This is a first step preparation in many dishes.
Chop - to cut something large into small pieces.
Consistency - the degree of firmness.
Cooking - the preparation of food by heating to the correct temperature to make food edible.
Deep fry - to cook by submerging food into at least 2 inches of very hot oil or other fat. Most often the oil is heated to 350 or 375 degrees. French fries are deep fried.
Dice - to cut into very small, uniform pieces.
Dough - the result of combining flour, liquid and other ingredients into a mass which can be kneaded either by hand or a special attachment on an electric mixer.
Drizzle - to lightly sprinkle drops of liquid over food.
Fillet - a piece of chicken, fish or beef without bones. To fillet is the procedure used to remove the bones.

Fold - to add a beaten ingredient that has been expanded by the incorporation of air into something that is heavier. This is usually done with a spatula and it is important to use a light touch so as not to deflate the air pockets.

Fry - to cook food in fat or oil. The fat remains in the pan after the dish is cooked and is not part of the final product being served.

Garnish - to decorate a dish after it has been cooked. If fresh herbs are used as a garnish, they should appear in the dish in the chopped form. For example, don't decorate a salad with basil leaves if no basil appears on the ingredient list.

Grate - to break up into small particles by rubbing against a metal or plastic device that has small, sharp holes in it (a grater). Cheese, potatoes, onions, carrots and apples are often grated.

Grill - a method of cooking using the dry heat process. When grilling, the heat source is beneath the food, as in cooking over an indoor or outdoor grill. When grilling, the meat, chicken or fish has attractive grill marks on its surface.

Marinade - the liquid used to tenderize and flavor foods before cooking.

Marinate - to tenderize and flavor food by covering with a liquid that contains some acid, such as lemon juice, vinegar or wine. Seasonings are often added to the liquid.

Measure - to dole out the proper amount called for in a recipe. Use measuring spoons and measuring cups for accurate work.

Mince - to cut into very fine pieces.

Mix - to combine ingredients.

Pan fry - to cook in a hot fat or oil. Unlike deep frying, the amount of fat is not measured in inches, but instead just covers the bottom of the pan. Hash browned potatoes are pan fried.

Peel - to remove the skins from fruits and vegetables.

Poach - to cook in simmering water to which either lemon juice, vinegar or wine has been added.

Puree - to mash to a smooth consistency.

Reduce - to boil off extra liquid.

Roasting - a method of cooking using the dry heat process.

Sauté - a method of cooking which uses a little oil or fat in the pan where the fat or oil is included in the final product. For example, onions are sautéed before other ingredients are added to the pan.

Sift - to remove lumps in flour or sugar by passing it through a sieve or strainer.

Simmer - to cook in a liquid below the boiling point. Usually the liquid is heated to 185-195 degrees and there is only a light movement on the surface of the liquid.

Steam - to cook over boiling water in a separate container so that the food does not touch the water.

Stew - to cook cut up pieces of meat, fish or chicken in a liquid.

Stir - to move ingredients around in a bowl or pan.

Stir-fry - to cook ingredients in a small amount of oil over very high heat with constant stirring until cooking is complete. The time required for cooking is usually a few minutes.

Whisk - to beat with a whip or whisk until ingredients are incorporated. Also, a metal tool used to combine liquids.

Zest - the peel of a citrus fruit. The zest does not include any of the bitter white part of the peel.

HOW LONG WILL THIS TAKE ?

The first question that busy people ask is "How long will I be in the kitchen?" I suggest that before you start cooking you read the recipe from beginning to end to get a feel of not only time involved, but also what ingredients and equipment are needed.

Every recipe in this book has an approximate time for preparation (organizing, chopping, preparing pans, initial sautéing, etc.) as well as for cooking. This time is shown on the clock face that accompanies each recipe, and is rounded to the nearest 15 minutes.

In some cases, however, there is no cooking involved, specifically in the case of some appetizers and salads, so only one clock face follows the recipe title.

Remember, everyone works at a different speed, and the more familiar you are with a recipe, the less time it will take.

Or, you might find that your time is much different from what I suggest, as does my daughter. Her cooking schedule often goes as follows: chop the onion, make a phone call, sauté the onion and garlic, make another phone call, change the CD, finish the recipe.

Breakfast

The critical period in matrimony is breakfast time.
A.P. Herbert

Apple Pecan Muffins

Makes 12   Prep   Cooking

Moist and delicious. Serve these warm or at room temperature. While the temptation might be to eat all these muffins at once, resist if you can and freeze some for later. It's wonderful to go to the freezer and have a convenient snack waiting.

½ cup chopped pecans
¼ cup flour
1 teaspoon baking soda
¼ teaspoon cinnamon
¼ teaspoon ground allspice
1/8 teaspoon salt
½ cup sugar
½ cup vegetable oil
1 egg
2 tablespoons lemon juice
1 teaspoon vanilla extract
2 cups grated tart green apple (2 large)

- Preheat oven to 350 degrees
- Lightly grease a muffin tin with vegetable spray or butter
1. Place pecans on a baking sheet and toast 8-10 minutes.
2. Combine flour, baking soda, cinnamon, allspice and salt in a medium bowl and mix gently.
3. In a large bowl combine the sugar, vegetable oil, egg, lemon juice and vanilla and whisk to blend.
4. Mix in dry ingredients, then the grated apple and pecans. Fill each muffin tin with 1/3 cup batter. Bake for 35 minutes, or until a cake tester comes out clean. Cool before serving.
Note: When squeezed, a large lemon has about 4 tablespoons of juice.

Great Morning Muffins

Makes 12   Prep 🕐   Cooking 🕐

Did you ever wonder what "healthy" tastes like? These are the
answer. A great way to start the day.

1 cup flour
½ cup bran cereal
½ cup toasted wheat germ
½ cup quick oatmeal
½ cup cornmeal
½ cup sugar
½ cup walnuts or pecans, chopped
½ cup raisins
2 teaspoons baking powder
1 teaspoon baking soda
1 teaspoon cinnamon
1 teaspoon ground ginger
1 teaspoon ground allspice
½ cup milk
½ cup unflavored yogurt
1/3 cup vegetable oil
1 tart green apple, grated
1 egg

- Preheat oven to 400 degrees
- Lightly grease a muffin tin with vegetable spray or butter

1. In a large bowl combine flour, bran cereal, toasted wheat
germ, oatmeal, cornmeal, sugar, walnuts or pecans, raisins,
baking powder, baking soda, cinnamon, ginger, and allspice.
2. In a small bowl whisk together the milk and yogurt. Add
the vegetable oil, grated apple and egg and combine.

3. Pour milk mixture over dry ingredients and stir until just combined.

4. Spoon ½ cup batter into each muffin tin. Bake 20 minutes or until a cake tester comes out clean. Cool before serving.

CBS (Carrot Banana Spice) Muffins

Makes 15   Prep   Cooking

Great for breakfast along with a big glass of juice and some fresh fruit.

1 cup whole wheat flour
½ cup flour
1 cup bran cereal
2 teaspoons cinnamon
1 teaspoon ginger
1 teaspoon baking soda
1 teaspoon baking powder
½ teaspoon ground allspice
¼ teaspoon ground cloves
1 teaspoon salt
½ cup raisins
½ cup shredded carrot (1 medium)
½ cup mashed banana (1 small)
2/3 cup unflavored yogurt
½ cup orange juice
2 tablespoons vegetable oil

- Preheat oven to 350 degrees
- Lightly grease muffin tins with vegetable spray or butter

1. In a large bowl combine the whole wheat flour, flour, bran cereal, cinnamon, ginger, baking soda, baking powder, allspice, cloves and salt. Make a well in the center.
2. In a small bowl combine the raisins, carrot, banana, yogurt, orange juice and vegetable oil. Pour into the well and fold into the dry ingredients.
3. Spoon ½ cup batter into each muffin tin. Bake 20 minutes or until tester inserted into centers comes out clean. Cool before serving.

Pumpkin Bread

Makes 2 loaves   Prep 🕐   Cooking.🕐

What would Thanksgiving be without Pumpkin Bread ? I had a friend who didn't know that pumpkin puree can be bought in a can so she cooked and pureed a pumpkin for her recipe, vowing never to go through this much trouble again, ever. When she found out about the miracle of canned pumpkin, she was somewhat embarrassed, to say the least.

4 eggs
1 cup vegetable oil
¾ cup orange juice
2 cups sugar
1 can (16 ounces) pumpkin
3½ cups flour
½ teaspoons salt
2 teaspoons baking soda
1½ teaspoons cinnamon
½ teaspoon ground cloves
1 teaspoon nutmeg
1 teaspoon ground allspice
½ cup raisins

- Preheat oven to 350 degrees
- Lightly grease two 9 inch loaf pans with vegetable spray or butter

1. In a large bowl beat the eggs until they are light colored. Blend in the vegetable oil, orange juice, sugar and the pumpkin.
2. Add the flour, salt, baking soda, cinnamon, cloves, nutmeg and allspice and beat until blended.
3. Stir in the raisins. Pour into prepared pans.
4. Bake 45 minutes or until a cake tester comes out clean.

Chocolate Chip Banana Bread

Makes 2 loaves   Prep   Cooking

Our daughter's friend has been making this banana bread for years. He bakes for friends' birthdays and always brings a few loaves for week-end trips. He's the only young man I know who smiles when he sees overripe bananas - it's the only excuse he needs to bake.

1 cup vegetable oil
2 cups sugar
3 eggs
2 teaspoons vanilla
3 cups flour
1 teaspoon baking soda
½ teaspoon baking powder
1 teaspoon salt
2 teaspoons cinnamon
2 cups mashed ripe banana (2 large)
2 cups chocolate chips

- Preheat oven to 325 degrees
- Lightly grease two 9 inch loaf pans with vegetable spray or butter
1. In a large bowl beat the oil with the sugar. Add the eggs and the vanilla and beat to combine.
2. In a small bowl combine the flour, baking soda, baking powder, salt and cinnamon. Add to the oil mixture.
3. Fold in the mashed banana and the chocolate chips. Pour into the prepared loaf pans.
4. Bake 1 hour, or until a cake tester comes out clean.

Breakfast Bran Shortcakes with Summer Fruit

Serves 4   Prep 🕐   Cooking 🕐

Perfect for a light summer brunch, these shortcakes are especially delicious and satisfying and make a spectacular presentation. They are also very easy to make. "Wow" is the most common response when these shortcakes are served.

1 cup bran cereal
3 tablespoons milk
½ cup flour
½ cup whole wheat flour
3 tablespoons sugar
2 teaspoons baking powder
1 teaspoon cinnamon
2 teaspoons orange zest *
3 tablespoons unsalted butter, room temperature
3 eggs, beaten to blend
3 cups mixed berries, sliced summer fruit or bananas
2 cups unflavored or fruit flavored yogurt

- Preheat oven to 400 degrees
- Lightly grease a baking sheet with vegetable spray or butter
1 In a small bowl combine bran cereal with milk and set aside to soften.
2. In another bowl, mix together the flour and the whole wheat flour, sugar, baking powder, cinnamon and orange zest. With a pastry blender or with your fingertips, cut in the butter until the mixture resembles coarse meal. Add the bran mixture and the eggs, and stir just to combine.

3. Divide the dough into 4 equal portions. Shape each portion into a 3 inch round and place on the prepared baking sheet. Bake 15 minutes, or until brown.

4. Cool 10 minutes. Slice horizontally. Spoon yogurt on bottom half, cover with fruit, replace top and serve.

Note: The shortcakes can be made ahead and reheated in a 350 degree oven until warm, about 7 minutes.

* See How To

Baked Honey Wheat Pancakes

Serves 4   Prep⏰   Cooking ⏰

Serve these with a yogurt fruit shake for an extra-healthy breakfast. These pancakes make life easy for the cook. The batter is poured into the pan, and all the work is done. No last minute standing at the griddle.

1 cup bran cereal
¼ cup wheat germ
½ teaspoon baking soda
½ teaspoon baking powder
½ teaspoon salt
½ cup hot water
¼ cup vegetable oil
¼ cup honey
1 cup flour
½ cup milk
½ cup unflavored yogurt
1 egg

Maple syrup
Sliced fresh fruit

- Preheat oven to 425 degrees
- Lightly grease a 15x10 inch jelly roll pan with vegetable spray or butter

1. In a large bowl combine bran cereal, wheat germ, baking soda, baking powder, salt, water, vegetable oil, honey and flour. Stir to soften cereal.
2. In a small bowl combine the milk, yogurt and egg. Beat to combine, add to the dry ingredients and blend.
3. Pour batter into the prepared pan and smooth with a spatula. Bake 8-10 minutes or until firm to the touch.
4. Cut into squares and serve with maple syrup and fresh fruit.

Baked French Toast with Sautéed Apples

Serves 3 or 4   Prep 🕑   Cooking 🕑

*This French toast is easier to make than the usual version.
Serve with warm maple syrup and sliced fresh fruit. For a
heartier breakfast, serve with sausage or bacon.*

2 tablespoons butter
6 slices day old French bread or Challah, 1 inch thick
4 eggs
2 cups milk
2 teaspoons vanilla
½ teaspoon cinnamon

Sautéed Apples (recipe follows)

1. Place the butter in a 9x13 baking pan and melt in a 350
degree oven or in a microwave oven. Remove pan from oven.
2. In a medium bowl combine the eggs, milk, vanilla and
cinnamon and whisk to blend.
3. Arrange bread slices in a single layer in the buttered baking
pan. Pour egg mixture over the bread. Let soak until all the
liquid is absorbed, turning once. This should take about 25
minutes.
4. Preheat oven to 400 degrees. Bake 25 minutes.

Sautéed Apples

2 tablespoons unsalted butter
3 large tart green apples, peeled, cored and cut into wedges
1 teaspoon ground allspice

1. Melt the butter in a medium skillet.
2. Add the apples and stir to coat. Sprinkle with the allspice.
Cook, while stirring, for 5 minutes or until the apples are tender
but still firm.

Breakfast Baked Apples

Serves 6   Prep   Cooking

Baked apples remind me of fall. These can be served warm or chilled. They aren't necessarily for breakfast only. When served with a dollop of frozen yogurt or creme fraiche, these baked apples make a great dessert.

6 large baking apples, such as Rome Beauty
1/3 cup granola
1/3 cup pitted dates, chopped
¼ cup pecans or walnuts, chopped
½ teaspoon cinnamon
½ teaspoon nutmeg
1 tablespoon lemon juice
2 tablespoons honey
¾ cup apple juice or water

• Preheat oven to 350 degrees
1. Core the apples, making a 1 inch cavity, and place in a baking dish that will hold the apples upright.
2. In a small bowl combine the granola, dates, pecans or walnuts, cinnamon, nutmeg and lemon juice. Spoon into the opening of each apple and pack in tightly.
3. Stir together the honey, apple juice or water. Pour over the apples.
4. Cover and bake for 30 minutes. Uncover and continue baking for 35 more minutes.
5. Serve warm or at room temperature.
Note: A melon baller is a useful tool for coring the apples.

Appetizers and Hors D'oeuvres

For when we lose twenty pounds, dear reader...we may be losing the twenty best pounds we have! We may be losing the pounds that contain our genius, our humanity, our love and honesty.   Woody Allen

Five Star Artichoke Spinach Dip

Serves 4   Prep😔   Cooking 😔

Our son's friends clamor for more when he serves this hot dip with blue corn tortilla chips and celery and carrot sticks. He says they claim he never makes enough of it - but they should know he's simply saving their appetites for dinner. I like this dip with cubes of French bread as an alternative to the chips. Be sure to wring all the water out of the spinach - best to do it in small handfuls.

1 jar (6 ounces) marinated artichoke hearts, drained
1 package (10 ounces) frozen chopped spinach, defrosted, and
    well drained
3 cups Pepper Jack cheese, shredded (about ¾ pound)
½ cup mayonnaise
½ cup white wine
1 teaspoon garlic salt

• Preheat oven to 350 degrees
1. Chop the artichoke hearts and combine with spinach and cheese in an ovenproof casserole.
2. In a small bowl combine the mayonnaise, white wine and garlic salt. Pour over the spinach and mix to combine.
3. Bake for 15 minutes.

Many Bean Dip

Makes 1 cup   Prep 🕐

Serve this dip with raw vegetables, pita wedges and tortilla chips. Bean dips are always popular, and this one is extra tasty.

½ cup sliced almonds
1 large clove garlic
2 tablespoons onion, roughly chopped
¼ cup parsley
1¼ cups cooked beans (use any combination of canned
    garbanzo, pinto and black beans to equal 1¼ cups)
2 tablespoons olive oil
1 tablespoon lemon juice
¼ cup unflavored yogurt
½ teaspoon cumin
½ teaspoon salt
¼ teaspoon pepper, freshly ground

1. Place almonds on a baking sheet and bake at 350 degrees about 7 minutes, or until the almonds are lightly browned and smell fragrant.
2. In a food processor or blender chop the garlic, onion and parsley. Add the beans, olive oil, lemon juice, yogurt, cumin, salt and pepper and process until smooth.
3. Add the almonds and process with a few on-off pulses to roughly chop the almonds.
4. Refrigerate 1 hour before serving.

Shrimp Dip

Makes 2 cups   Prep 🕐

Serve with crackers or thinly sliced baguette. If tiny shrimp are unavailable, dice medium size shrimp or use fresh crab.

8 ounces cream cheese
¼ cup unflavored yogurt
1 tablespoon lemon juice
½ teaspoon crushed red pepper flakes
¼ cup green bell pepper, diced
¼ cup red bell pepper, diced
½ cup celery, diced
5 green onions, sliced
½ pound bay shrimp
Salt and pepper, freshly ground

1. With a wooden spoon, beat together the cream cheese and yogurt. Stir in the lemon juice, red pepper flakes, red and green bell pepper, celery and green onions.
2. Gently fold in shrimp. Season with salt and pepper. Refrigerate 2 hours before serving.

Clam Dip

Makes 1 cup   Prep ⏲

This long time favorite can be served with crackers and fresh vegetables.

3 ounces cream cheese, room temperature
2 tablespoons unflavored yogurt
2 tablespoons finely chopped celery
¼ teaspoon salt
1/8 teaspoon pepper, freshly ground
1 teaspoon Worcestershire sauce
1 can (6 ounces) chopped clams, drained and juices reserved

1. In a small bowl beat together the cream cheese and yogurt. Add the celery, salt, pepper and Worcestershire.
2. Add the clams and 1 tablespoon of the reserved clam juice and mix.
3. Refrigerate 2 hours.

Spinach Dip

Makes 2 ½ cups   Prep 🕐

Be sure to wring all the water out of the spinach. It's best to do it in small handfuls. Serve with crackers and fresh veggies.

1 package (10 ounces) frozen chopped spinach, thawed and
   well drained
½ cup chopped parsley
8 green onions, chopped
1 can water chestnuts (8 ounces), rinsed, drained and chopped
1 cup mayonnaise
1 cup unflavored yogurt
1 teaspoon garlic salt
½ teaspoon pepper, freshly ground

1. In a small bowl combine spinach, parsley, green onions and
water chestnuts.
2. Add the mayonnaise, yogurt, garlic salt and black pepper
and fold in. Refrigerate 2 hours before serving.

Hummus

Makes 1 cup   Prep 🕐

Serve this, or the no oil version, with sliced pita bread and assorted fresh vegetables. It's also wonderful spread on a turkey sandwich with lettuce, tomatoes and thinly sliced cucumber or on a vegetarian sandwich. Tahini, which is sesame seed paste, can be purchased at a natural foods store.

1 can (15 ounces) garbanzo beans, rinsed and drained
4 large garlic cloves
½ cup parsley, packed
½ cup tahini
½ cup fresh lemon juice (about 2 large lemons)

1. Place the garbanzo beans, garlic, parsley, tahini and lemon juice in a food processor or blender. Process until smooth.
2. Refrigerate 2 hours before serving.

Hummus, Updated

Makes 1 cup   Prep ⏱

This version has no added oil. It's not the original Mid-Eastern version, but it's equally tasty and is a big seller at our local outdoor farmer's market.

1 can (15 ounces) garbanzo beans, rinsed and drained
4 large garlic cloves
½ cup parsley, packed
1 teaspoon soy sauce
1/8 teaspoon cumin
3 tablespoons fresh lemon juice
1 tablespoon water

1. Place garbanzo beans, garlic, parsley, soy sauce, cumin, lemon juice and water in a food processor or blender. Process until smooth. Add a little more water if necessary.
2. Refrigerate 2 hours before serving.

Black Bean and Corn Salsa

Makes 5 cups   Prep ⏱

Serve with tortilla chips. This salsa is also a nice accompaniment to grilled fish or chicken.

1 can (15 ounces) black beans, rinsed and drained
2 cups frozen corn, defrosted
1 tomato, seeded and diced
6 green onions, chopped
Juice of 2 limes
5 tablespoons olive oil
1 teaspoon cumin
1 teaspoon garlic salt

1. In a medium bowl combine the black beans, corn, tomato and green onions.
2. In a small bowl whisk together the lime juice, olive oil, cumin and garlic salt. Pour over the vegetables and mix gently.
3. Refrigerate at least 1 hour.

Salsa Mexicana

Makes 4 cups   Prep 🕐

Freshly made salsa is easy to make and beats store bought hands down. When removing the seeds of any chili pepper, use a teaspoon and be careful not to get the seeds on your hands. The smaller varieties are the hottest. The Anaheim chili used in this recipe, however, is long, green and mild.

3 medium tomatoes, seeded and diced
¼ cup chopped onion
¼ cup chopped cilantro
1 Anaheim chili pepper, seeded and diced
1 large clove garlic, minced
1 tablespoon red wine vinegar
½ teaspoon dried oregano
½ teaspoon salt
1/8 teaspoon pepper, freshly ground

1. Place the diced tomato in a bowl.
2. Add the onion, cilantro, Anaheim chili pepper, garlic, vinegar, oregano, salt and pepper. Gently toss.
3. Refrigerate several hours.

Guacamole

Makes 2 cups   Prep ⏱

To keep the guacamole from turning brown before serving, place the avocado pit in the middle of the dip and cover with plastic wrap. I don't know why it works, but it does! For a special presentation, serve with a basket of white, yellow and blue corn chips.

2 ripe avocados
1 small tomato, seeded and diced
Juice of 1 lime
3 green onions, chopped
1/8 teaspoon Tabasco

1. Cut avocados in half. Remove the pits. Using a large serving spoon scoop the avocado pulp out of the skin and place in a small bowl. Mash, using a fork. The consistency should be uneven; leave some small chunks of avocado.
2. Add the diced tomato, lime juice, green onions and Tabasco.
3. Refrigerate 1 hour before serving.

Teriyaki Cheese Spread

Makes 1 cup   Prep 🕑

This cheese spread has a unique taste. People can't figure out what's in it. Serve with assorted crackers.

1 package (8 ounces) cream cheese, room temperature
3 green onions, minced
1 teaspoon soy sauce
1 tablespoon minced fresh ginger *
1 tablespoon dry sherry

1. Combine the cream cheese, green onions, soy sauce, ginger and sherry. Turn into a serving dish.
2. Refrigerate 2 hours or overnight.
* See How To

Roasted Garlic

Serves 6   Prep   Cooking 🕐

Couldn't be easier to make! Why this appetizer is so pricey on restaurant menus has always been a mystery to me. Serve with lots of thinly sliced, crusty French bread and perhaps a wedge of Brie. There are two different ways of preparing roasted garlic: one keeps the whole head intact, and the other roasts the individual peeled cloves. I prefer the second method because it is less messy to serve.

2 large heads garlic, cloves separated and peeled *
2 teaspoons olive oil

1 baguette, sliced

- Preheat oven to 400 degrees.
1. Place the garlic in a small ovenproof dish. Drizzle with the olive oil. Cover the dish with aluminum foil.
2. Bake about 25 minutes or until the garlic is very soft when pierced with a knife. Cool.
3. Serve with the baguette and have guests spread a roasted clove onto the sliced bread.
* See How To

Alpine Loaf

Serves 8   Prep 🕐   Cooking 🕐

Very much like cheese fondue, this appetizer brings to mind a ski lodge and a great day in the snow. The bread shell can be cut into wedges (and devoured) after the dip is finished.

1 round loaf French bread (1 pound)
½ cup unflavored yogurt
½ cup sour cream
3 tablespoons onion soup mix
1 tablespoon flour
¼ cup beer or white wine
3 cups Swiss cheese, shredded (about ¾ pound)

1. Cut a thin slice off the top of the bread. Hollow out the center, leaving a 1 inch shell. Cut soft bread center into 1 inch cubes and reserve.
2. In a large saucepan combine the yogurt, sour cream, onion soup mix, flour and beer or wine. Add the cheese, stir to combine and simmer over low heat, stirring constantly, until melted, about 4 minutes.
3. Pour into the bread shell and serve immediately with the bread cubes.
Note: The bread shell with the cheese in it can be kept warm in a 300 degree oven for about ½ hour.

Baguette Pizza

Serves 12   Prep   Cooking

People of all ages devour these mini pizzas. Be sure to make lots since they seem to disappear. For a great lunch, spread the pizza mixture on baguette halves and bake as directed.

1 can (4 ounces) diced green chilies
1 can (2 ounces) chopped ripe olives
1 can (8 ounces) sliced mushrooms, drained
4 green onions, chopped
1 can (8 ounces) tomato sauce
1 teaspoon sugar
1½ cups grated Cheddar or Monterey Jack cheese
    (about 1/3 pound)
¼ cup vegetable oil

2 baguettes, sliced in ¼" rounds

• Preheat oven to 400 degrees
1. In a medium bowl combine the green chilies, ripe olives, mushrooms, green onions, tomato sauce, sugar, Cheddar or Monterey Jack cheese and vegetable oil.
2. Just before serving spread pizza mixture on sliced baguette.
3. Bake 10 minutes or until the mixture is bubbly.

Pesto Pizza

Serves 4-6   Prep 🕑   Cooking 🕑

These pizzas are also wonderful for a quick lunch or for a special first course. Sliced mushrooms, olives, roasted red bell pepper strips or sliced red onion can be added with the tomatoes.

4 individual size pizza crusts
4 tablespoons pesto, purchased or homemade (see p. 97)
4 ounces Havarti cheese, thinly sliced
2 tomatoes, thinly sliced
2 cups Mozzarella cheese, shredded (about ½ pound)
¼ cup grated Parmesan cheese

• Preheat oven to 400 degrees
1. Place pizza crusts on baking sheet. Spread pesto over crusts and layer with Havarti cheese, then the tomatoes. Cover with Mozzarella and Parmesan cheeses.
2. Bake 10 minutes, or until topping bubbles.
3. Cut into wedges.
Note: Use freshly grated Parmesan in all your cooking. Buy it at the deli counter in convenient plastic containers. It is far superior to that which is sold in a shaker container.

Spinach Balls with Yogurt Dip

Makes 1 dozen   Prep   Cooking

These spinach balls can be made ahead and frozen. When freezing individual items, such as these spinach balls, place on a cookie sheet and put them in the freezer for an hour. (I need to set a timer because I'm likely to forget them and find them perhaps days later.) Place the now frozen items in a zip lock baggie. If you put them in a baggie without first freezing individually, you will wind up with a solid mass!

1 package (10 ounces) frozen chopped spinach, thawed
1 egg
3 green onions, diced
½ cup dried bread crumbs
¼ cup Parmesan cheese, freshly grated
2 teaspoons lemon juice
¼ teaspoon cumin
½ teaspoon salt
¼ teaspoon pepper

¼ cup unflavored yogurt
½ teaspoon Dijon mustard
1/8 teaspoon cayenne pepper

- Preheat oven to 400 degrees.
- Lightly grease a baking sheet with vegetable spray or oil
1. Squeeze the spinach dry in small handfuls.
2. In a medium bowl lightly beat the egg. Add the spinach, green onions, bread crumbs, Parmesan, lemon juice, cumin, salt and pepper.
3. Roll into 12 balls. Place on the prepared baking sheet and bake for 12 minutes.
4. Meanwhile, combine the yogurt, Dijon and cayenne. Serve with the warm spinach balls.

Garlic and Onion Bread Strips

Serves 8   Prep 🕒   Cooking 🕒

This is a quick and easy version of garlic bread. I like it as an hors d'oeuvre or with a meal.

1 baked cheese pizza crust or flat bread (16 ounces)
½ cup mayonnaise
½ cup Parmesan cheese
6 green onions, diced
5 garlic cloves, minced
1 teaspoon dried basil
1 teaspoon dried thyme
1 teaspoon dried oregano

- Preheat oven to 400 degrees
1. Place pizza crust on baking sheet.
2. Combine mayonnaise, Parmesan, green onions, garlic, basil, thyme and oregano. Spread evenly over the crust.
3. Bake 15 minutes. Cut into 2 inch strips and then into smaller rectangles.
Note: Freshly grated Parmesan can be purchased at the deli counter.

Best Ever Cornbread

Serves 8   Prep   Cooking

This cornbread, a big favorite in my cooking classes, is so delicious that it is perfect just as it is, served as an hors d'oeuvre. Or, it can be cut into larger squares to serve in place of bread with lunch or dinner.

1½ cups flour
1¼ cups cornmeal
¾ cup sugar
½ teaspoon baking powder
½ teaspoon baking soda
½ teaspoon salt
2 eggs
½ cup vegetable oil
¾ cup milk
¼ cup unflavored yogurt
1 cup cream style corn (from an 8 ½ ounce can)
½ cup grated sharp Cheddar cheese (about 1/8 pound)
1 can (4 ounces) mild green chilies

- Preheat oven to 325 degrees
- Grease a 9 inch square pan with butter or vegetable spray

1. In a large bowl combine the flour, cornmeal, sugar, baking powder, baking soda and salt.
2. In a medium bowl whisk to combine the eggs, vegetable oil, milk and yogurt. Stir in the cream style corn, Cheddar cheese and green chilies.
3. Add the egg mixture to the dry ingredients and stir until just combined.
4. Pour the batter into the prepared pan. Bake for 1 hour. Cut into squares and serve warm.

Note: This can be made ahead and reheated. For convenience, cut into squares before warming in the oven.

Black Bean and Corn Quesadillas

Serves 4   Prep 🕑   Cooking 🕑

Quesadillas make great appetizers, snacks or even a light lunch or dinner. They can be embellished with sour cream and salsa.

2 teaspoons vegetable oil
8 large flour tortillas
2 cups grated Monterey Jack cheese (about ½ pound)
1 cup black beans, rinsed and drained, from a 14 ounce can
1 cup frozen corn (no need to defrost)

1. Heat ½ teaspoon oil in a large skillet over medium heat. Place 1 flour tortilla in the pan and sprinkle with ½ cup of the cheese, ¼ cup black beans and ¼ cup of the corn. Cover with a second tortilla.
2. Cook until the cheese begins to melt and the bottom tortilla begins to brown, about 2 minutes. Using a spatula, turn over and cook an additional 2 minutes.
3. Remove to a cutting board and cut into 6 wedges. Serve immediately. Continue with remaining tortillas, cheese, beans and corn.

Soups

Cooking is like love. It should be entered into with abandon or not at all. Harriet Van Horne

Shrimp, Rice and Broccoli Chowder

Serves 4-6   Prep   Cooking

Make this comforting soup in just a few minutes. Serve with a salad and warm bread for a quickly assembled dinner.

1 cup rice
2 tablespoons vegetable oil
1 small onion, chopped
½ pound mushrooms, sliced
2 cups frozen chopped broccoli, defrosted and patted dry
1 red bell pepper, chopped
½ teaspoon dried thyme
2 cups chicken broth
2 cups milk
1 can (17 ounces) cream style corn
½ pound bay shrimp
Salt and pepper, freshly ground

1. Cook the rice and set aside. *
2. Meanwhile, heat the oil in a large pot over medium heat. Slowly sauté the onion, until soft but not brown, about 4 minutes. Increase heat, add the mushrooms and cook until the mushrooms change color, about 3 more minutes.
3. Add the broccoli, red bell pepper and thyme and cook for 3 minutes.
4. Stir in the chicken broth, milk and cream style corn and cook, uncovered, for 10 minutes, until hot.
5. Remove from the heat, add the bay shrimp and the rice, cover, and let sit 3 minutes. Add salt and pepper to taste.
Note: Canned chicken broth is a good alternative to homemade.
* See How To

Chicken Curry Soup

Serves 4   Prep 🕐   Cooking 🕐

Lots of home cooks have this recipe. I don't know where it first appeared. I love this main dish soup! I'd come home on a winter evening, starving of course, and in no time at all the kitchen would be smelling so good and dinner would be ready.

2 tablespoons oil
1 small onion, diced
1 teaspoon curry powder
1 teaspoon cumin
1 teaspoon dried oregano
½ cup rice, uncooked
3 carrots, cut into ¼ inch rounds
6 cups chicken broth
4 skinless, boneless, chicken breast halves, cut into 1 inch cubes
2 zucchini, cut into ¼ inch rounds
1 can (15 ounces) chopped tomatoes, drained

Lime wedges

1. Heat the oil in a large pot and slowly sauté the onion until soft, but not brown, about 4 minutes. Add the curry powder, cumin and oregano and cook for 1 minute until the flavors are released.
2. Add the rice and carrots and stir well. Cover with the chicken broth, bring to a boil, reduce heat, cover and simmer until the rice and carrots are tender, about 15 minutes.
3. Add the chicken cubes and continue to simmer for 5 minutes until the chicken is cooked.
4. Add the zucchini and tomatoes and cook for 5 minutes more.
5. Serve with a lime wedge to squeeze over each portion.

Chinese Vegetable Soup

Serves 4   Prep 🕑   Cooking 🕑

This soup is a perfect starter for an Asian style meal.

6 cups chicken broth
1 cup sliced mushrooms
1 cup broccoli florets
1 cup bean sprouts
3 tablespoons soy sauce
3 tablespoons cider vinegar
2 tablespoons Asian sesame oil
½ teaspoon pepper, freshly ground
2 tablespoons cornstarch mixed with ¼ cup water
1 egg, beaten
7 ounces tofu, cut into ½ inch cubes
3 green onions, chopped

1. Pour the broth into a medium size pot and add the mushrooms, broccoli florets, bean sprouts, soy sauce, cider vinegar, sesame oil and pepper. Stir to combine and simmer for 10 minutes.
2. Increase the heat to medium high and add the cornstarch mixture. Cook for 3 minutes, stirring occasionally, until the soup is thickened.
3. Stir the soup in one direction and slowly drizzle in the egg. When the egg is set, add the tofu. Remove from the heat and let sit, covered, 2 minutes.
4. Garnish with the green onions.

Hearty Split Pea Soup

Serves 8   Prep   Cooking ⏲

An old time, vegetarian, family favorite. Like most soups, this freezes well.

½ cup split peas
½ cup barley
8 cups water
3 carrots, sliced
2 stalks celery, sliced
1 small onion, chopped
1 bay leaf
1 teaspoon dried thyme
1/8 teaspoon cayenne pepper
2 teaspoons salt
¼ teaspoon pepper, freshly ground

Toast squares or croutons

1. In a large pot combine the split peas, barley, water, carrots, celery, onion, bay leaf, thyme, cayenne pepper, salt and pepper. Bring to a boil, lower the heat and cook, covered, for 1 hour, or until the peas are very soft.
2. Discard bay leaf, puree the solids in a food processor or blender with a little of the liquid and add back to the broth in the pot. Stir to incorporate.
3. Garnish with toast squares or croutons.

Lentil Chard Soup

Serves 6   Prep   Cooking

Serve this delicious, hearty soup on a cold winter night. This soup has been a big favorite in my cooking classes.

1½ cups lentils, rinsed and picked over for stones
8 cups water
4 beef bouillon cubes
1 medium potato, scrubbed and cubed
1 package (10 ounces) frozen Swiss chard, defrosted and juices
     reserved
4 tablespoons olive oil
1 medium onion, chopped
1 bunch cilantro, stems removed, chopped
4 large garlic cloves, minced
1 teaspoon salt
½ teaspoon pepper, freshly ground
½ teaspoon cumin
3 tablespoons lemon juice

1 lemon, sliced in rounds

1. In a large pot combine the lentils, water, beef bouillon cubes, potato and Swiss chard with the defrosted liquid. Bring to a boil, cover and reduce heat. Cook for 40 minutes.
2. Meanwhile, heat the olive oil in a small frying pan and sauté the onion until soft but not brown, about 4 minutes. Add the cilantro and the garlic and sauté 1 more minute. Set aside.
3. After the soup has simmered the 40 minutes add the contents of the frying pan along with the salt, pepper, cumin and lemon juice. Cover the pot and let sit for 5 minutes.
4. Serve garnished with a lemon slice in each bowl.

Carrot Chutney Soup

Serves 4   Prep 🕐   Cooking 🕐

This soup is delicious and unusual - perfect for a dinner party, but easy enough to make for a week day supper. I recently bought a hand blender and am amazed at how easy it is to puree directly in the soup pot. When using a hand blender, be sure not to lift the blade above the level of the soup while it is turned on, unless you would like to take a carrot soup bath, that is!

1 tablespoon vegetable oil
1 small onion, chopped
6 large carrots (1½ pounds), pared and thinly sliced
1 stalk celery, chopped
1 small potato, peeled and cubed
5 cups chicken broth
¼ cup bottled peach chutney

1. In a medium size pot heat the oil over moderate heat. Add the onion and sauté until soft but not brown, about 4 minutes.
2. Add the carrots, celery and potato and cook 3 minutes. Add the chicken broth, bring to a boil, reduce heat and simmer, covered, for 20 minutes.
3. Puree the vegetables with a little bit of the broth in a food processor or blender. Return the puree to the broth remaining in the saucepan. Add the chutney and mix well to incorporate. Serve hot or at room temperature.
Note: Chutney can be purchased in a specialty food store.

Broccoli Apple Soup

Serves 4   Prep 🕐   Cooking 🕐

Easy to make and very low in fat.

1 bunch broccoli, tough stalk ends discarded, chopped
2 tablespoons butter
½ cup onion, chopped
1 tart apple, peeled, cored and chopped
4 cups chicken broth
1 teaspoon salt
½ teaspoon pepper, freshly ground

Unflavored yogurt
Diced Apple, for garnish

1. Set aside 1 cup broccoli florets for garnish.
2. In a medium size pot melt the butter and sauté the onion over moderate heat until soft. Add the broccoli and the apple and cook 3 more minutes.
3. Pour the chicken broth over the vegetables and bring to a boil. Reduce heat, cover and simmer 20 minutes, or until the broccoli is very tender.
4. Meanwhile, bring a small pot of water to a boil. Add the reserved broccoli florets. Blanch for 15 seconds. Drain and set aside.
4. Puree the vegetables with a little of the broth in a food processor or blender. Return to the saucepan and season with the salt and pepper. Heat briefly.
5. Garnish with yogurt, the apple and broccoli florets.

Mushroom and Potato Soup

Serves 6   Prep   Cooking

I won a First Prize with this recipe in a cooking contest. It's a great soup and loved by all. (It's also pretty terrific to win a contest.)

1 tablespoon butter *plus* 1 tablespoon butter
3 leeks, cleaned and chopped *
2 large carrots, sliced
6 cups chicken broth
2 teaspoons dried dill weed
1 teaspoon salt
¼ teaspoon pepper, freshly ground
1 bay leaf
2 pounds russet potatoes, scrubbed, cut into 1 inch
     cubes
1 pound small mushrooms, cleaned and halved *
¼ cup flour
1 cup milk or half and half

Sour cream or unflavored yogurt for garnish

1. Melt 1 tablespoon butter in a large pot over medium heat. Sauté leeks and carrots until tender, about 5 minutes.
2. Add chicken broth, dill weed, salt, pepper, bay leaf and potatoes. Bring to a boil, reduce heat, cover and simmer until the potatoes are tender, about 20 minutes.
3. Meanwhile, melt the remaining 1 tablespoon butter in a large skillet. Sauté the mushrooms over high heat until golden, about 5 minutes.

4. In a small saucepan that is off the heat, whisk together the flour and ¼ cup of the milk. Slowly whisk in the remainder of the milk. Then place the saucepan over moderate heat and continue whisking until the mixture thickens, occasionally using a spatula to scrape up any flour that might be sticking to the bottom of the saucepan. Add to the simmering soup when the potatoes are tender and gently mix to combine.

5. Add mushrooms. Remove the bay leaf. Garnish each serving with sour cream or yogurt, if desired.

Note: Use a large skillet when sautéing the mushrooms so they will brown, rather than steam in their own juices.

* See How To

Tucson Corn Chowder

Serves 4   Prep   Cooking 🕐

Another quick soup - perfect served with flour tortillas or perhaps Black Bean and Corn Quesadillas.

1 tablespoon butter
1 small onion, diced
1 stalk celery, thinly sliced
2 cans (17 ounces each) cream style corn
1 cup milk
1 cup chicken broth
1 medium carrot, very thinly sliced
¼ teaspoon pepper, freshly ground

1. In a medium size pot melt the butter over moderate heat and sauté the onion and celery until soft, but not brown, about 4 minutes.
2. Add the cream style corn, milk, chicken broth, carrot and pepper. Simmer, uncovered, for 20 minutes. Stir occasionally.

Mexican Vegetable Soup

Serves 8   Prep 🕐   Cooking 🕐

A perfect soup to warm the soul on a cold, rainy day. This splendid soup does take about an hour to make, but it is well worth the time spent. Like most other soups, this one also freezes well.

½ cup rice
1 large yam, peeled and cut into ½ inch cubes
4 cups water
1 can (15 ounces) black beans, rinsed and drained
1 can (15 ounces) kidney beans, rinsed and drained
½ cup frozen corn
¼ cup raisins
1/3 cup chopped parsley
1 teaspoon honey
2 beef bouillon cubes
3 tablespoons oil
1 large onion, chopped
4 garlic cloves, minced
3 carrots, sliced in rounds
1 small green bell pepper, chopped
2 celery stalks, sliced
1½ teaspoons MEXICAN SPICE MIX (recipe follows)
1 can (46 ounces) tomato juice
1 can (15 ounces) chopped tomatoes

MEXICAN SPICE MIX
Combine:
1½ teaspoons ground coriander
1 teaspoon cumin
1 teaspoon curry powder
½ teaspoon ground pepper
½ teaspoon cayenne
2 teaspoons dried oregano

1. Cook the rice and set aside. *
2. Meanwhile, in a large pot combine the yam and water.
Bring to a boil, reduce heat and cook until the yam is almost
tender, about 10 minutes. Add the black beans, kidney beans,
corn, raisins, parsley, honey and beef bouillon cubes. Simmer
10 more minutes.
3. In a large skillet heat the oil and sauté the onion and garlic
until tender but not brown. Add carrots and sauté 3 more
minutes. Add bell pepper, celery and 1½ teaspoons MEXICAN
SPICE MIX. Mix well and cook 4 more minutes. (Save the
remainder of the MEXICAN SPICE MIX for a later use.)
4. Add to the soup pot the sautéed vegetables, the tomato juice
and the chopped tomatoes with their liquid. Simmer 30
minutes.
5. Just before serving add the rice. Add water if the soup gets
too thick.
*Note: It's easy to tell the difference between a sweet potato
and a yam. Simply scratch the peel with your fingernail. A
sweet potato's flesh will be dark orange and a yam's flesh light
orange.*
* See How To

Lentil Vegetable Soup

Serves 6   Prep   Cooking 🌓 🌓

I like to serve this soup in large bowls with baskets of warm bread. It makes a perfect vegetarian dinner when accompanied by a green salad.

2 tablespoons oil
1 large onion, chopped
3 cloves garlic, chopped
1 green bell pepper, chopped
8 cups water
3 cans (8 ounces each) tomato sauce
1½ cups lentils, rinsed and picked over for stones
1 cup brown rice, uncooked
1 cup dry white wine or chicken stock
3 carrots, sliced
3 celery stalks, sliced
2 large red potatoes, scrubbed and diced
1 teaspoon dried thyme
1 teaspoon dried basil
2 teaspoons salt
½ teaspoon pepper, freshly ground

1. In a large pot heat the oil. Add the onion and garlic and sauté until soft, but not brown, about 4 minutes. Add the bell pepper and sauté another 3 minutes.
2. Add the water, tomato sauce, lentils, brown rice, wine or chicken stock, carrots, celery, potatoes, thyme, basil, salt and pepper.
3. Cover and simmer until the lentils and rice are tender and the soup is thick, about 1 hour and 15 minutes. Stir occasionally during the cooking.
Note: The rice and lentils absorb lots of liquid, so add some water to thin the soup if it becomes too thick.

Salad Dressings and Salads

After a good dinner, one can forgive anybody, even one's own relations. Oscar Wilde

Basic Vinaigrette

Makes ¾ cup   Prep 🕐

This classic dressing can keep for two weeks, refrigerated.

1 tablespoon Dijon mustard
3 tablespoons red or white wine vinegar
½ cup olive oil
Salt and pepper

1. In a small bowl whisk together the Dijon mustard and the vinegar.
2. Slowly whisk in the olive oil. Add salt and pepper to taste.

Honey Mustard Vinaigrette

Makes ¾ cup   Prep 🕐

When using honey, dip the measuring spoon in oil before measuring out the honey; then the honey won't stick to the spoon.

2 tablespoons honey
2 tablespoons white wine vinegar
1 tablespoon Dijon mustard
2 teaspoons dried thyme
2 teaspoons lemon juice
½ cup olive oil

1. In a small bowl whisk together the honey, white wine vinegar, Dijon, thyme and lemon juice.
2. Slowly whisk in the oil. Refrigerate for up to two weeks.

Creamy Herb Salad Dressing

Makes 1 cup   Prep 🕐

This creamy dressing stays good in the refrigerator for a week.

1/3 cup mayonnaise
1/3 cup unflavored yogurt
1 tablespoon honey
2 tablespoons white wine vinegar
1 teaspoon Dijon mustard
½ teaspoon pepper, freshly ground
¼ teaspoon garlic salt
½ teaspoon dried oregano

1. In a small bowl whisk together the mayonnaise, yogurt and honey.
2. Add in the vinegar, Dijon mustard, pepper, garlic salt and oregano and whisk to combine.

Bleu Cheese Salad Dressing

This salad dressing is thick and delicious. It takes a minute to make, is so much tastier than the bottled variety and can be refrigerated for up to a week.

Makes 1¾ cups   Prep 🕑

¾ cup mayonnaise
¾ cup unflavored yogurt
4 ounces Bleu cheese
1 clove garlic, minced or pressed
1 teaspoon Worcestershire sauce
1 teaspoon lemon juice
¼ teaspoon salt
1/8 teaspoon pepper, freshly ground

1. In a small bowl whisk together the mayonnaise and the yogurt.
2. Add the Bleu cheese, garlic, Worcestershire sauce, lemon juice, salt and pepper and gently combine.

A Great Green Salad:

Use a combination of different greens such as iceberg, romaine, spinach, napa cabbage, savoy cabbage, and red leaf lettuce. Wash the lettuces ahead and have them chilled. Add some of the following:

Chopped or shredded carrots, sliced celery, sliced radishes, red or green bell pepper strips, sliced red or green onion, sliced tomatoes or whole cherry tomatoes, blanched green beans, rinsed and drained canned garbanzo, kidney or black beans, sliced pickled beets, black olives, marinated artichoke hearts, sliced hearts of palm, shredded Cheddar, Jack or Swiss cheese, crumbled Bleu or Feta cheese, sunflower seeds, raisins and croutons.

To make this into a main dish meal, add diced chicken or roast beef, canned tuna or freshly cooked shrimp.

Toss with the dressing of your choice just before serving.

New Caesar Salad

Serves 4   Prep 🕑

Does anyone really know where Caesar salad originated? One story tells of a restaurant owner in Tijuana, Mexico who named this salad after himself in the 1920's. Another tells of its first being served in southern California in the 1940's. Whatever the true story, Caesar salad has been a favorite of diners for years. Today cooks have been adding grilled chicken or shrimp to the salad to turn it into a main dish meal. This version eliminates the uncooked egg that is in the classic version.

CROUTONS:
1½ cups sourdough or French bread cubes with the crust
1 tablespoon olive oil
½ teaspoon garlic salt

SALAD:
1 large head Romaine lettuce, washed, chilled and torn into bite
    size pieces
2 large garlic cloves, minced or pressed
3 tablespoons lemon juice, freshly squeezed
2 teaspoons anchovy paste
½ teaspoon Worcestershire sauce
½ cup olive oil
¼ teaspoon pepper, freshly ground

¼ cup grated Parmesan cheese

FOR CROUTONS:
1. In a large skillet heat the olive oil over medium heat. Brown the croutons, turning several times, until they are golden brown.
2. Remove pan from the heat. Sprinkle with the garlic salt. Cool the croutons in the pan.

FOR SALAD:

1. In a large salad bowl combine the romaine lettuce and croutons.
2. In a small bowl whisk to combine the garlic, lemon juice, anchovy paste and Worcestershire sauce. Slowly whisk in the olive oil and the pepper.
3. Toss the lettuce and croutons with about half of the dressing and the Parmesan cheese. Add more dressing as needed. Serve immediately.

Note 1: Anchovy paste is packaged in a tube and can be found in the canned seafood section of the grocery store. Refrigerate after opening.

Note 2: Try something different, and substitute mini slices of Parmesan for the grated Parmesan. Buy a small wedge of Parmesan and shave enough to measure ¼ cup on the side slats of the hand grater, or shave the cheese with a vegetable peeler. This is a very contemporary presentation and actually makes the salad even more delicious.

Southwest Chicken Salad

Serves 4   Prep 🕐   Cooking 🕑

This salad was inspired after a visit to the Southwest. I like to make it early in the day to serve on a warm summer evening. Be sure to use a small spoon when removing the seeds from the jalapeno and take care not to get the seeds on your skin.

2 cups water
1 cup brown rice
2 whole chicken breasts, cooked *
1 tomato, seeded and diced *
1 small green bell pepper, sliced
1 cup frozen corn, thawed
1 can (15 ounces) black beans, rinsed and drained
4 green onions, sliced
3 tablespoons white wine vinegar
1 tablespoon Dijon mustard
1 jalapeno pepper, minced *
1/3 cup chopped parsley
1¼ teaspoons cumin
¾ teaspoon salt
¾ teaspoon pepper
½ cup olive oil

1. Bring 2 cups of water to boil in a small saucepan. Mix in brown rice and bring back to a boil. Cover pot, reduce heat to low and cook until the rice is tender and all the water is absorbed, about 30 minutes. Set aside to cool.
2. Cut the chicken into 1 inch cubes.
3. In a large bowl combine the rice, chicken, tomato, bell pepper, corn, black beans and green onions.
4. In a small bowl combine the vinegar, Dijon mustard, jalapeno pepper, parsley, cumin, salt and pepper. Slowly whisk in olive oil. Pour dressing over salad and toss to combine.
5. Refrigerate 2 hours before serving.
* See How To

Curry Yogurt Chicken Salad

Serves 6   Prep 🕐   Cooking 🕐

Another main dish salad for a hot summer day. Serve with Apple Pecan Muffins.

1 cup unflavored yogurt
3 tablespoons sour cream
2 teaspoons curry powder
1 teaspoon cumin
1 teaspoon dried thyme
1 teaspoon salt
2 tablespoons lemon juice, freshly squeezed
3 whole chicken breasts, cooked *
½ cup currants or raisins
1 large carrot, grated
2 stalks celery, thinly sliced
2 tart apples, cubed

1. In a small bowl combine the yogurt, sour cream, curry powder, cumin, thyme, salt and lemon juice.
2. Cut the chicken into 1 inch cubes.
3. In a large bowl combine the chicken, currants or raisins, carrot, celery and apple. Toss with the yogurt dressing.
4. Refrigerate several hours before serving.
Note: When celery is sliced or diced, there is no need to scrape it first since the "strings" that are sometimes bothersome in a whole stalk are no trouble when the piece of celery is small.
* *See How To*

Ginger Rice Salad

Serves 8 - 10   Prep🕐   Cooking🕐

This was a huge favorite at a Berkeley, California deli. I served this salad at a luncheon for 100 people and just about everyone requested the recipe. To make this into a main dish salad, add cubed, cooked chicken, turkey or roast beef.

4 cups brown rice
1 cup wild rice
8 cups water
4 beef bouillon cubes

½ cup tarragon vinegar
½ cup grated fresh ginger *
1/3 cup Dijon mustard
1 tablespoon salt
1 teaspoon pepper
1 cup olive oil
1 red bell pepper, chopped
1 green bell pepper, chopped
1 cup frozen peas, defrosted
6 green onions, chopped

1 cup chopped almonds, toasted *

1. Combine the brown and wild rice with the water and bouillon cubes. Bring to a boil, cover and simmer until all the water is absorbed, about 30 minutes. Turn out into a large bowl while still warm.

2. Combine the tarragon vinegar, ginger, Dijon mustard, salt and pepper. Slowly whisk in the olive oil. Pour over the warm rice and mix well.

3. Add the red and green bell peppers, frozen peas, green onions and chopped almonds. Mix well and refrigerate at least 2 hours before serving.

Note: If made many hours ahead, add the almonds just before serving.

* See How To

Corn Salad

Serves 6   Prep 🕐

I like to serve this salad with grilled chicken or hamburgers. What is it about cilantro that people either love it or hate it? I love it, but I also know several people who don't. This is a salad for cilantro lovers; of course, the cilantro can be eliminated, and the salad is still good.

2 cups frozen corn, defrosted
1 red onion, sliced
2 zucchini, diced
2 celery stalks, sliced
1 green bell pepper, chopped
½ cup cilantro leaves
2 garlic cloves
¼ cup red wine vinegar
1 tablespoon sugar
½ teaspoon salt
½ teaspoon pepper, freshly ground
2/3 cup olive oil

1. In a large bowl combine the corn, red onion, zucchini, celery and green bell pepper.
2. In a food processor or blender chop the cilantro and garlic. Add the red wine vinegar, sugar, salt and pepper and whirl until combined. Slowly add the olive oil.
3. Toss the vegetables with the dressing.
4. Refrigerate several hours.
Note: Cilantro, also known as Chinese parsley, has a similar appearance to Italian parsley and watercress. Ask the produce manager at the grocery store to point out the differences. Taste a leaf of each. Although they look alike, the flavors are very different and they shouldn't be used interchangeably.

French Potato Salad

Serves 8   Prep   Cooking

Makes a nice alternative to the usual mayonnaise based version. The red skinned potatoes contrast nicely with the parsley and green onions.

2½ pounds red skinned potatoes, cut into large dice, cooked *
1/3 cup chopped parsley
2 stalks celery, chopped
6 green onions, chopped
½ cup white wine vinegar
1 tablespoon Dijon mustard
2 cloves garlic, minced or pressed
1 teaspoon salt
¼ teaspoon pepper, freshly ground
2/3 cup olive oil

1. Place warm potatoes in a large bowl. Add parsley, celery and green onion.
2. In a small bowl combine the vinegar with the Dijon mustard, garlic, salt and pepper. Slowly whisk in the olive oil. Pour over the potatoes while they are warm. Gently toss to coat the potatoes.
3. Refrigerate for 4 hours.
* See How To

Coleslaw, Deli-Style

Serves 8   Prep 🕐

A must for a barbecue. The horseradish adds a nice subtle change to this popular salad. Why make this when it can be purchased at any deli? It takes less time to make it than it does to drive to the store, the taste is fresher, and it costs considerably less.

1 small head green cabbage, shredded (8 cups)
3 carrots, grated
½ cup chopped parsley
1 cup mayonnaise
¼ cup apple cider vinegar
1 tablespoon sugar
1 teaspoon salt
2 tablespoons prepared horseradish

1. In a large bowl combine the cabbage, carrots and parsley.
2. In a small bowl mix together the mayonnaise, apple cider vinegar, sugar, salt and horseradish. Pour over the cabbage and toss gently.
3. Refrigerate several hours.

Red Cabbage Coleslaw

Serves 8   Prep 🕐

My friend Charlotte warns that if you bring this to an annual gathering your friends will insist that you always bring it - and you'll never get to try new salad recipes!

½ small head red cabbage, shredded
½ small head green cabbage, shredded
1 small red onion, finely chopped
1 large carrot, grated
¾ cup red wine vinegar
½ cup sugar
1 teaspoon dry mustard
1 teaspoon celery seed
1½ teaspoon salt
1 cup vegetable oil

1. In a large bowl combine the red and green cabbage, red onion and carrot.
2. In a small pot combine the vinegar and sugar and bring to a boil to dissolve the sugar. (Or, in a microwave oven, heat the vinegar and sugar for 1 minute on high power.) Remove from the heat and add the dry mustard, celery seed and salt and whisk to combine. Add the oil and whisk again.
3. Pour warm dressing over the vegetables and gently toss. Refrigerate several hours or overnight.

New York Health Salad

Serves 8   Prep 🕙

*This coleslaw version first gained popularity in New York in the
'60's. My Dad traveled to work by bus and then the subway. After
work he would often stop at the deli/bakery that was right by the
bus stop and bring home some goodies. Health Salad was one of
our favorites. After I moved to California, I craved the fresh taste
of this salad and was lucky to get the recipe from my aunt's friend.
The first time I made it I felt as if I were revisiting my childhood.*

1 small head green cabbage, shredded
2 carrots, shredded
1 green bell pepper, thinly sliced
1 red bell pepper, thinly sliced
2 cucumbers, peeled and very thinly sliced
1 medium onion, thinly sliced
4 tablespoons sugar
3 tablespoons warm water
6 tablespoons vegetable oil
1½ teaspoons garlic salt
1½ teaspoons salt

1. In a large bowl combine the cabbage, carrots, green and red bell
peppers, cucumber and onion.
2. In a small bowl dissolve the sugar in the warm water. Whisk in
the oil, garlic salt and salt. Pour over the vegetables and mix well.
3. Refrigerate several hours before serving.

Protein Salad With Fruit

Serves 1   Prep 🕑

Here's a quick and easy lunch. Great to bring to work with a muffin or bagel. It's the right amount of food to calm my growling stomach, but not too much food to make me sleepy. It's also so easy to put together in the morning.

2 cups cottage cheese
¼ cup unflavored yogurt
1 teaspoon lemon juice
½ cup pecans, chopped
½ cup raisins or currants
1 apple, diced
1 banana, sliced
1 tablespoon toasted wheat germ

1. Mix all ingredients and serve on a bed of lettuce.

Protein Salad with Veggies

Serves 1   Prep 🕑

Here's another version of a great, quick, lunch salad.

2 cups cottage cheese
¼ cup unflavored yogurt
1 carrot, chopped
4 radishes, chopped
1 stalk celery, chopped
¼ cup cucumber, chopped
1 tablespoon sunflower seeds
Salt and pepper to taste

1. Mix all ingredients and serve on a bed of lettuce.

Chinese Asparagus Salad

Serves 6   Prep ⏰   Cooking ⏰

I love spring and fresh asparagus. The frozen and canned versions just don't compare. Buy a bunch of asparagus that has either all thin or all thick asparagus so they will cook through in the same length of time. Be sure not to overcook the asparagus; they should be slightly crunchy. And, most important, remember not to throw the woody ends into the garbage disposal. They clog the mechanism and it is a real chore to clean it out, sometimes even requiring a visit from the plumber.

1½ pounds asparagus, washed and trimmed *
2 cups water
2 tablespoons soy sauce
1 tablespoon vegetable oil
1 teaspoon Asian sesame oil
1 teaspoon white wine vinegar
1 teaspoon sherry
1 tablespoon grated fresh ginger *
1/8 teaspoon Tabasco
1/8 teaspoon sugar
2 tablespoons sesame seeds, toasted

1. Place the asparagus in a large skillet, cover with the water and cook over moderate heat, covered, until crisp tender, about 4 minutes. Drain and cool.
2. In a small bowl combine the soy sauce, vegetable oil, sesame oil, white wine vinegar, sherry, ginger, Tabasco and sugar.
3. Pour the dressing over the asparagus and refrigerate for 1 hour.
4. Place sesame seeds in a small skillet over medium heat and stir occasionally until they begin to brown. This takes about 4 minutes. Sprinkle over asparagus just before serving.
* See How To

Garden Bulgur Salad

Serves 8-10   Prep 🕑

The vegetables add crunch and color to this version of Tabbouli, a Middle Eastern salad. Leftovers are still delicious several days later.

2 cups bulgur (cracked wheat)
3 cups boiling water
2 large tomatoes, seeded and chopped *
3 zucchini, sliced into ¼ inch rounds
4 green onions, sliced
1 jar (4 ounces) roasted red bell pepper, drained and sliced
½ pound Feta cheese, crumbled
1 jalapeno pepper *
1 cup cilantro leaves
1 cup mint leaves
5 tablespoons white wine vinegar
¾ cup olive oil

1. Pour boiling water over the bulgur and let sit for 30 minutes until all the water is absorbed.
2. In a large bowl combine the tomatoes, zucchini, green onions, roasted red bell pepper and Feta cheese.
3. Cut the jalapeno in half and carefully remove the seeds with a teaspoon. In a food processor or blender pulse to combine the jalapeno, cilantro, mint leaves and the white wine vinegar. With the machine running, slowly add the olive oil.
4. Combine the bulgur with the vegetables. Add the dressing a little at a time and toss gently. Garnish with additional mint leaves.
Note: Bulgur can be found in the grain section of the grocery store, or in specialty food stores.
* *See How To*

Pear Cheddar Salad

Serves 8   Prep 🕐

A great fall salad to make when pears are in season. Buy the pears several days ahead to ripen. Best when served right after preparation. Toasted pecans or walnuts can be added just before serving.

6 ripe pears, unpeeled, cored and cut into 1 inch cubes
½ pound sharp Cheddar cheese, cut into ½ inch cubes
1 bunch cilantro, washed well and stems removed
¼ cup diced red onion

3 tablespoons lemon juice
1 tablespoon Dijon mustard
½ cup olive oil
½ teaspoon salt
¼ teaspoon pepper, freshly ground

1. In a large bowl place the pears, Cheddar cheese, cilantro and red onion.
2. In a small bowl combine the lemon juice and Dijon mustard. Whisk in the olive oil, then add the salt and pepper.
3. Pour dressing over salad and gently toss.
4. Refrigerate 1 hour.

Tomato Basil Mozzarella Salad

Serves 4   Prep 🕐

Summer means one thing to me: fresh, vine ripened tomatoes. If you don't have a garden, be sure to find a farmer's market and fill your basket; get fresh basil there, too. Fresh Mozzarella is available at lots of delis these days; I prefer to use fresh, water packed Mozzarella for salads.

6 large tomatoes, seeded and cut into 1 inch cubes *
½ pound Mozzarella, cubed
1 cup basil leaves, chopped
2 tablespoons olive oil
3 tablespoons Balsamic vinegar
1 clove garlic, minced or pressed
1 teaspoon dried oregano
1 teaspoon sugar
1 teaspoon salt
½ teaspoon pepper, freshly ground

1. In a large bowl combine the tomatoes, Mozzarella and basil leaves.
2. In a small bowl whisk to combine the olive oil, Balsamic vinegar, garlic, oregano, sugar, salt and pepper.
3. Pour over tomatoes and Mozzarella and toss gently.
* See How To

Bulgarian Tomato Salad

Serves 4   Prep 🕑

Another salad to be made with summer's vine ripened tomatoes. Best when served the same day as prepared.

4 large tomatoes, seeded and cut into 1 inch cubes *
1 cucumber, peeled, sliced lengthwise, then cut in ¼ inch slices
1 jar (7 ounces) roasted red bell pepper, drained and chopped
4 green onions, chopped
2 tablespoons red wine vinegar
1 tablespoon olive oil
¾ teaspoon salt
1/8 teaspoon pepper, freshly ground
4 ounces Feta cheese, crumbled

1. In a large bowl combine the tomatoes, cucumber, red bell pepper and green onion.
2. In a small bowl combine the red wine vinegar, olive oil, salt and pepper. Pour over the vegetables and toss gently.
3. Just before serving add the Feta cheese.
* See How To

Spicy Peanut Pasta Salad

Serves 4   Prep 🕐   Cooking 🕐

This salad is perfect by itself or as part of a meal. Some people like to heat the leftovers for a warm noodle dish, or to add cooked chicken or shrimp to the cold or warm version.

½ pound noodles, preferably ¼ inch wide fettucine noodles
½ cup chunky peanut butter
¼ cup rice wine vinegar
¼ cup water
3 tablespoons soy sauce
1 tablespoon sesame oil
2 tablespoons honey
2 cloves garlic, minced or pressed
2 teaspoons grated ginger *
1 cup bean sprouts
1 carrot, shredded
6 green onions, sliced

1. Cook the noodles in boiling water. Drain, rinse well, and pat dry with paper towel.
2. In a large bowl whisk to combine the peanut butter, rice wine vinegar, water, soy sauce, sesame oil, honey, garlic and ginger.
3. Add the noodles, bean sprouts, carrot and green onion. Mix well and refrigerate 1 hour before serving.
Note 1: Be sure to measure out the sesame oil before measuring out the honey; if oil is on the spoon the honey won't stick to it.
Note 2: Rice wine vinegar is found in the Asian section of the grocery store. By itself, it makes a great non-fat salad dressing.
* *See How To*

Quinoa, Apple and Pear Salad

Serves 4-6   Prep 🕑   Cooking 🕑

Quinoa, called the "Mother Grain" by the Incas, is very high in protein, easy to digest, and loved by both natural food fans and gourmets. It can be purchased in a health food store.

1 cup quinoa
2 cups water
¼ cup orange juice
4 teaspoons lemon juice
1 teaspoon raspberry vinegar
¼ cup olive oil
1 tablespoon chives, chopped
1 tablespoon parsley, chopped
Salt and pepper
1 tart apple, cut into ¼ inch dice
1 pear, cut into ¼ inch dice
¼ cup currants
3 tablespoons sliced almonds, toasted *

1. Rinse the quinoa well and place in a small saucepan. Cover with the 2 cups of water. Bring to a boil, reduce heat, cover and simmer for 15 minutes, or until all the water is absorbed.
2. In a small bowl combine the orange juice, lemon juice and raspberry vinegar. Slowly whisk in the olive oil. Add the chives and parsley, and salt and pepper to taste.
2. In a medium bowl combine the quinoa with the diced apple and pear and the currants. Toss with the dressing.
3. Chill several hours. Just before serving, sprinkle with the toasted almonds.
* See How To

New Age Waldorf Salad

Serves 4   Prep

For a delicious lunch, try this salad with a cup of soup and a muffin.

1 small jicama, peeled and cut into 1 inch cubes
1 Delicious apple, cut into 1 inch cubes
1 Pippin apple, cut into 1 inch cubes
2 stalks celery, thinly sliced
½ cup currants
¼ cup pitted dates, chopped

¼ cup mayonnaise
¾ cup unflavored yogurt
2 tablespoons lemon juice
2 teaspoons grated ginger *
½ teaspoon cinnamon

½ cup Spanish peanuts

1. In a medium bowl combine the jicama, apples, celery, currants and dates.
2. In a small bowl combine the mayonnaise, yogurt, lemon juice, ginger and cinnamon. Whisk to combine.
3. Pour the dressing over the fruit and gently toss.
4. Add the Spanish peanuts just before serving.

*   See How To

Pasta

I saw him even now going the way of all flesh, that is to say towards the kitchen. John Webster

About Pasta

1. How much pasta to cook? Usually one pound serves four people for dinner, or six to eight for an appetizer course.
2. To cook pasta, bring a large pot of water to a boil. Add a teaspoon or two of oil, and slowly add the pasta so that the water maintains the boil. Stir occasionally. Time varies according to shape of the pasta, and if the pasta is fresh or dry. Drain as soon as the pasta is *al dente,* or somewhat firm to the bite.
3. Don't rinse the pasta under water after draining; not rinsing helps the sauce to stick to the pasta.
4. Reheat leftover, plain pasta by dropping into a pot of boiling water and cooking for about a minute.
5. Leftover plain pasta can also be frozen. To reheat, drop into a pot of boiling water for about 2 minutes, stirring a few times.

San Francisco Seafood Pasta

Serves 6   Prep 🕑   Cooking 🕑

Delicious! For a variation try substituting a firm fleshed white fish, such as halibut or snapper, for the shrimp or scallops.

3 tablespoons olive oil
1 small onion, chopped
5 cloves garlic, minced or pressed
1 teaspoon crushed red pepper
1 can (28 ounces) crushed tomatoes
2 cans (4 ounces each) chopped clams, juices reserved
4 tablespoons chopped parsley
1 teaspoon dried basil
6 ounces shrimp, peeled and deveined *
6 ounces scallops
Salt and pepper

1 pound pasta, cooked and drained

1. Heat oil in a large heavy skillet over medium heat. Add onion and garlic and sauté until the onion is soft but not brown, about 4 minutes. Add the crushed red pepper and cook 1 minute more.
2. Mix in tomatoes with their liquid, the reserved clam juice, parsley and basil. Cover skillet and cook over medium low heat for 15 minutes. Uncover and continue simmering until some of the sauce is cooked off, stirring occasionally, 15 more minutes.
3. Increase heat to medium and add the clams, shrimp and scallops and cook until the shrimp and scallops are cooked through, about 4 minutes. Season with salt and pepper.
Note: The best way to tell if shellfish is cooked through is to remove one piece from the pot and cut it in half. It should be uniform in color and not translucent.
* See How To

Eggplant Mushroom Pasta

Serves 4   Prep 🕐   Cooking 🕐

This is a favorite of eggplant lovers. Pass some freshly grated Parmesan or Pecorino cheese to sprinkle over the top and serve some crusty French bread and a green salad.

2 tablespoons olive oil
1 small onion, diced
5 cloves garlic, minced
½ pound mushrooms, sliced (2 cups)
½ teaspoon crushed red pepper
1 small eggplant, unpeeled, cut into 1 inch cubes
1 red bell pepper, chopped
1/3 cup red wine
1 can (15 ounces) chopped tomatoes
1 teaspoon dried oregano
1 teaspoon salt
¼ teaspoon pepper, freshly ground

1 pound fettucine or other pasta, cooked and drained

1. In a large bottomed saucepan heat the oil. Over medium heat sauté the onion and garlic until the onion is soft but not brown, about 4 minutes.
2. Add the mushrooms and crushed red pepper and sauté until the mushrooms begin to brown, about 3 minutes.
3. Add the eggplant and red bell pepper and sauté 3 minutes.
4. Add the red wine, chopped tomatoes, oregano, salt and pepper. Reduce the heat to medium low, cover and simmer 30 minutes.
5. Remove the cover and cook an additional 10 minutes to thicken the sauce.

Note: Pecorino cheese is made from sheep's milk, is a hard, grating cheese like Parmesan, and is a very tasty alternative to grated Parmesan or Romano.

Pasta, Mediterranean Style

Serves 4   Prep 🕑   Cooking 🕑

Inspired by a love of artichoke hearts and hearts of palm, this pasta is easy to put together and is a sure winner. The sauce takes just about the same time to cook as does the pasta. So if time is a problem, first put the pasta water on to boil and then start the sauce.

2 tablespoons olive oil
½ cup chopped onion
4 garlic cloves, minced or pressed
2 jars (6 ounces each) marinated artichoke hearts, drained
1 can (7 ounces) hearts of palm, sliced in rounds
2 tablespoons anchovy paste
1 can (6 ounces) pitted whole black olives, drained
1 red bell pepper, thinly sliced

1 pound angel hair or other pasta, cooked and drained

1. In a large skillet heat the oil. Sauté the onion and garlic over moderate heat until the onion is soft but not brown.
2. Add the artichoke hearts, hearts of palm, anchovy paste, olives and red bell pepper. Stir and cook until hot, about 4 minutes.
3. Serve over the pasta.
Note 1: Hearts of palm, which used to be considered exotic, are now found as condiments at the most casual salad bars. The cans are located in the canned vegetable section in the grocery store. Note 2: Anchovy paste is packaged in a tube and found with the canned fish. Refrigerate after opening.

Pesto Fettucine with Chicken

Serves 4   Prep 🕑   Cooking 🕑

Leftovers are delicious served at room temperature. If asparagus is unavailable, substitute green beans or broccoli florets.

2 tablespoons olive oil
1 red bell pepper, cut into thin strips
½ pound asparagus, cut into 1 inch pieces*
4 boneless chicken breast halves, cut into ½ inch strips
½ cup pesto, purchased or homemade (recipe follows)

1 pound fettuccine, cooked and drained

1. In a large skillet heat 1 tablespoon of the olive oil. Add the red bell pepper strips and the asparagus and cook over moderate heat, stirring occasionally, until softened, about 5 minutes. Transfer to a large bowl and cover to keep warm.
2. Heat the remaining 1 tablespoon oil in the skillet. Sauté the chicken over medium heat until cooked through, about 5 minutes.
3. Return the vegetables to the skillet and toss briefly to rewarm.
4. In a large bowl combine the pasta with the contents of the skillet and the pesto. Mix well and serve immediately.

* See How To

Quick and Easy Pesto

Use this pesto for Pesto Fettucine with Chicken , or just by itself with cooked pasta. Or, add some blanched* veggies to cold pasta and toss with the pesto for a tasty pasta salad.

Makes 1½ cups   Prep

2 cups fresh basil leaves
½ cup pine nuts or walnuts
½ cup parsley
1 cup grated Parmesan cheese
½ teaspoon salt
¼ teaspoon pepper
½ cup olive oil

1. In a food processor or blender combine the basil leaves, nuts, parsley, Parmesan, salt and pepper. Slowly add the oil.
Note: Leftover pesto can be stored in the freezer. Spoonfuls are wonderful stirred in hearty soups, such as Minestrone
* *See How To.*

Pasta Puttanesca

Serves 4   Prep   Cooking

Translated as "Lady of the Night" Pasta, this is another recipe that seems to appear on many restaurant menus. Lots of people claim they don't want to even be in the same room as an anchovy, but don't let these little fish keep you away from this sauce. They add a unique and salty flavor and are the subtle heart of this dish. Serve this sauce over baked chicken, with a side dish of pasta, for another version.

4 cloves garlic
6 anchovy fillets, drained
3 tablespoons olive oil
1 can (28 ounces) crushed tomatoes
1 can (4 ounces) chopped black olives
1 tablespoon capers
1/8 teaspoon pepper, freshly ground

1 pound spaghetti, cooked and drained

1. Finely chop together the garlic and anchovy fillets.
2. Heat the olive oil in a medium saucepan. Gently sauté the garlic and anchovies for 3 minutes. Add the tomatoes and black olives and simmer covered 30 minutes, stirring occasionally.
3. Add the capers and black pepper and serve over the pasta.

Stuffed Shells

Serves 4   Prep   Cooking

Serve these shells with a green salad for a comfort food, family style dinner.

12 jumbo shells, cooked and drained

1 can (14 ounces) tomato puree
1 teaspoon dried basil
1 teaspoon sugar
1 teaspoon salt
½ teaspoon pepper, freshly ground
1 tablespoon olive oil
1 small onion, chopped
1 clove garlic, minced or pressed
½ pound ground turkey or ground beef
1 package (10 ounces) frozen chopped spinach, thawed and well
    drained
2 tablespoons grated Parmesan cheese
½ cup cottage cheese

• Preheat oven to 350 degrees
1. In a small bowl, combine tomato puree, basil, sugar, salt and
pepper. Set aside.
2. In a medium skillet, heat the olive oil. Sauté the onion and
garlic until the onion is soft but not brown. Add the ground
turkey or ground beef and brown. Drain off any drippings. Add
½ cup tomato puree mixture, the spinach, Parmesan cheese and
cottage cheese, mix and cook for 2 minutes.
3. Fill each cooked shell with 2 tablespoons of the meat mixture.
Place stuffed shells in a 9 inch square pan.
4. Combine the remaining meat sauce with the remaining
tomato puree and pour over the shells. Cover with foil and bake
45 minutes.

Baked Penne with Vegetables

Serves 4   Prep 🕐   Cooking 🕐

Here's a pasta casserole that isn't tomato based. It is wonderful for a casual supper. Like all casseroles, the work is done ahead, making this another winner for a pot luck.

½ pound penne pasta, cooked and drained

1 tablespoon olive oil
½ small onion, diced
2 cloves garlic, minced or pressed
½ pound mushrooms, sliced (2 cups)
2 cups frozen chopped broccoli, defrosted
1 cup frozen peas, defrosted
1½ tablespoons lemon zest, minced *
½ teaspoon dried oregano
3 tablespoons flour
1¾ cups milk
1 teaspoon salt
¼ teaspoon pepper, freshly ground
¼ teaspoon nutmeg
½ cup grated Parmesan cheese

• Preheat oven to 350 degrees
1. In a large skillet heat the oil and slowly sauté the onion and garlic until soft but not brown. Increase the heat and add the mushrooms and sauté 4 more minutes. Stir in the broccoli, peas, lemon zest and oregano and set aside.
2. In a small saucepan, off the heat, whisk together the flour and ¼ cup of the milk. Slowly whisk in remaining milk, place over high heat and bring to a boil, whisking constantly. Add salt, pepper and nutmeg. Reduce the heat and cook until the sauce thickens, about 3 minutes. Cool slightly.

3. In a large bowl combine the pasta, sauce and the contents of the skillet. Turn into a casserole dish and sprinkle with the Parmesan.

4. Bake for 35 minutes, uncovered, or until the sauce is bubbly.

Note: Always use freshly grated Parmesan, and stay far away from what is called 'Parmesan cheese' and is sold in cans or jars; any resemblance in flavor or texture is purely fictitious! You can buy Parmesan grated at the deli counter, or you can keep a small wedge in the refrigerator, wrapped in plastic, and grate when you need it.

* See How To

Vegetable Pasta Casserole

Serves 8   Prep   Cooking

I have brought this casserole to many pot luck dinners and, I modestly admit, it was always the favorite. It's well worth the extra time it takes to assemble. It can be assembled a day ahead, refrigerated, and baked right before serving.

10 ounces ziti pasta, cooked and drained
1 tablespoon olive oil

2 medium carrots, thinly sliced in rounds
1 bunch broccoli, cut into florets; the stems into slices
3 tablespoons olive oil
5 cloves garlic, minced or pressed
1 large zucchini, thinly sliced into rounds
1 teaspoon salt
¼ teaspoon pepper, freshly ground
½ cup white wine
1 cup ricotta cheese
¼ cup TOMATO SAUCE FOR PASTA CASSEROLE (recipe follows)
1 egg, beaten
2 tablespoons chopped parsley
1 teaspoon dried basil
3 cups Mozzarella cheese, grated (about ¾ pound)

1. Cook the ziti in lots of boiling water, drain, and toss with the oil. Tossing with the oil prevents the ziti from sticking to itself.
2. Drop carrots and broccoli into boiling water and cook until crisp tender, about 1 minute. Drain and towel dry.
3. In a large skillet heat the oil. Sauté the carrot, broccoli, zucchini and garlic for 3 minutes. Add the salt, pepper and the wine and cook 3 more minutes. Cool.

4. In a large bowl combine the ricotta, ¼ cup of the tomato sauce, egg, parsley, basil and half of the Mozzarella. Mix in the pasta and the vegetables.

5. Preheat oven to 350 degrees. Turn into a 9x13 casserole. Top with remaining tomato sauce and the remaining Mozzarella. Bake for 40 minutes.

Note: If bringing a casserole to a pot luck dinner, take the casserole out of the oven just before you leave. Cover with foil, then wrap it in several sheets of newspaper. The casserole will stay warm for almost an hour.

Tomato Sauce for Vegetable Pasta Casserole

3 tablespoons olive oil
3 cloves garlic, minced or pressed
1 can (15 ounces) crushed tomatoes in puree
2 teaspoons dried basil
1 tablespoon chopped parsley
½ teaspoon salt
¼ teaspoon pepper, freshly ground

1. Heat oil in a saucepan over moderate heat. Add the garlic and stir 1 minute, being careful not to let the garlic brown.

2. Add the crushed tomatoes, basil, parsley, salt and pepper.

3. Bring to a boil, stirring constantly. Reduce heat and simmer until the sauce thickens, about 15 minutes.

Sausage and Peppers Pasta

Serves 4   Prep 🕐   Cooking 🕐

This a is quick and easy pasta dish for the hurried and the hungry. It takes only moments to put together.

2 tablespoons olive oil
2 green bell peppers, sliced
1 onion, sliced
4 turkey sausages, cut into 1 inch rounds
1 can (15 ounces) chopped tomatoes, drained
1 teaspoon dried oregano

1 pound ziti or other pasta, cooked and drained

1. Heat the olive oil in a large skillet. Sauté the peppers and onion over medium heat until they are soft, about 4 minutes. Remove to a platter.
2. Lightly brown the sausage in the oil that is remaining in the skillet. This should take 3 minutes.
3. Return the peppers and the onions to the skillet. Add the tomatoes and the oregano, cover and simmer gently for 15 minutes.
4. Remove the cover and cook an additional 5 minutes to thicken the sauce.

Meat

There is one thing more exasperating than a wife who can cook and won't, and that's a wife who can't cook and will.
Robert Frost

About Meat

1. Purchase meat that is well trimmed of fat.
2. Beef should be bright red in color and lamb should be pinkish.
3. When buying ground meat, always buy the leanest grade possible.
4. Refrigerate as soon as possible after a trip to the store, and use within a day or two. If buying meat for later use, over wrap the store wrapped package in either aluminum foil or freezer paper. Label and date the package. Meat should be good for up to six months, but the quality goes down over time.
5. Slowly defrost frozen meat in the refrigerator in order to retain the natural juices.

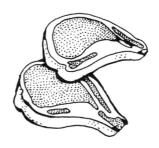

Mama's Meatballs

Serves 6-8   Prep 🕐   Cooking 🕐

*These meatballs have been a family favorite for many years.
Young men can eat massive amounts. Serve with pasta or in a
hollowed out French roll for a delicious hot meatball sandwich.
Sautéed peppers and onions added to the sandwich make this
unbeatable. It takes about an hour to make these meatballs; turn
on some opera, nibble on some breadsticks and enjoy the
wonderful aromas. Freeze leftover meatballs for later use.*

5 slices day-old sweet French bread, crusts removed
1 pound ground turkey
1 pound lean ground beef
1 cup grated Parmesan cheese
1 large onion, chopped
½ cup chopped parsley
1 teaspoon salt
½ teaspoon pepper, freshly ground
1 teaspoon dried oregano
2 teaspoons dried basil
3 cloves garlic, minced or pressed
3 eggs, lightly beaten

MAMA'S TOMATO SAUCE (recipe follows)

1. In a food processor or blender, whirl bread to make crumbs.
2. In a large bowl, mix together crumbs, ground turkey, ground
beef, Parmesan cheese, onion, parsley, salt, pepper, oregano,
basil, garlic and eggs. Blend well. Form mixture into 1½ inch
meatballs.

3. Preheat broiler. Lay meatballs in a large roasting pan and broil 4 inches from the heat, until browned. Do not turn. Remove from pan and drain on paper towels.

4. Add meatballs to sauce. Bring to a boil, reduce heat and cover. Simmer for 45 minutes.

Mama's Tomato Sauce

1 can (28 ounces) tomato puree
1 can (28 ounces) crushed tomatoes
3 cloves garlic, minced or pressed
½ cup chopped parsley
¾ cup red wine
2 tablespoons dried basil
1 tablespoon dried oregano
2 teaspoons salt
½ teaspoon pepper, freshly ground
1 teaspoon sugar
1½ cups water

1. In a medium saucepan combine the tomato puree, crushed tomatoes, garlic, parsley, red wine, basil, oregano, salt, pepper, sugar and water.
2. Bring to a boil, and add the meatballs. Reduce heat and simmer, covered, 45 minutes.

Stuffed Cabbage Rolls

Serves 4   Prep 🕑   Cooking 🕑

Grandma made the best stuffed cabbage. I loved watching her roll up the cabbage leaves. She was such a tidy and efficient worker. My mother once tried a new recipe for stuffed cabbage that was in the local newspaper. Each roll was tied up with thread! It took her all day to tie these little packages. She served it to us with little scissors for snipping the thread. Needless to say, she went back to Grandma's recipe the next time. This is best made a day ahead. It also freezes well.

1 large green cabbage
1 pound lean ground beef
1 pound ground turkey
2 eggs, lightly beaten
¼ cup diced onion
¼ cup diced carrot
½ teaspoon salt
Juice of 1 large lemon
½ cup brown sugar
1 can (8 ounces) tomato sauce
½ cup raisins

1. Bring a large pot of water to a boil. Remove the core of the cabbage and immerse the cabbage in the water. Remove after 4 minutes and carefully peel off the outer leaves and set aside. Return the cabbage to the water and repeat until all the large leaves are removed. Roughly chop the remaining leaves.
2. Combine the ground beef, ground turkey, eggs, onion, carrot and salt.

3. Cut off the tough top section and the ribs of the larger leaves. Place a small ball of the meat mixture in the center of a leaf and fold the cabbage around it, completely enclosing the meat. Repeat with all the leaves. If there is extra meat, make small meatballs and add to the pot.

4. Place the chopped leaves on the bottom of a large saucepan. Place the rolls, seam side down, in the pan. Make two layers of the cabbage rolls, if necessary.

5. In a small bowl combine the lemon juice, brown sugar, tomato sauce and raisins. Pour over the cabbage rolls. Bring to a boil, reduce heat to low, and simmer, covered, 1 hour.

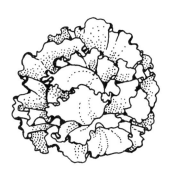

Middle Eastern Lamb

Serves 4-6   Prep 🕐   Cooking 🕐

Be sure to marinate a day ahead. Serve with Lentil Vegetable Casserole. Leftovers are quite delicious sliced very thin on a sandwich - use fresh, crusty bread for a real treat.

1 cup unflavored yogurt
4 cloves garlic, minced or pressed
1 tablespoon grated fresh ginger *
1 teaspoon cumin
1 teaspoon turmeric
1 teaspoon salt
¼ teaspoon cayenne pepper
2 pounds boneless lamb (ask the butcher to butterfly a half leg of
    lamb), fat removed

1. Mix together the yogurt, garlic, ginger, cumin, turmeric, salt and cayenne pepper. Pour over the lamb and marinate for 8 hours in the refrigerator, covered.
2. Remove lamb from refrigerator 1 hour before cooking.
3. Preheat the broiler and set the rack 4 inches from the heat source. Broil for 10 minutes, turn the lamb and cook for an additional 10 minutes, for medium rare. Let sit for 5 minutes, tented with aluminum foil , before slicing on the diagonal.
Note: A zip lock baggie works well for marinating. Place the lamb in the bag, then spoon in the marinade, being sure to cover all the meat. Remove all the air before closing.
* See How To

Curry Lamb in Pita Bread

Serves 4   Prep 🕐   Cooking 🕐

Think of this as a Middle Eastern version of Sloppy Joes.

1 pound lean ground lamb
1 small eggplant, unpeeled, cut into ½ inch cubes
1 medium onion, chopped
1 small green bell pepper, chopped
1 can (15 ounces) chopped tomatoes
1 teaspoon curry powder
½ teaspoon allspice
½ teaspoon nutmeg
1 teaspoon garlic salt
¼ teaspoon pepper, freshly ground

4 large Pita breads, halved
Unflavored yogurt

1. In a large skillet brown the lamb over moderate heat. Add the eggplant, onion and green bell pepper and cook, stirring often until the vegetables begin to soften, about 3 minutes.
2. Stir in the tomatoes with their liquid, curry powder, allspice, nutmeg, garlic salt and pepper. Bring to a boil, reduce heat to low, and simmer, covered, for 35 minutes.
3. Remove cover and cook 10 more minutes.
4. Spoon into the Pita bread and pass the yogurt.

Picnic Flank Steak

Serves 4   Prep 🕐   Cooking 🕐

Here's a simple marinade that helps to tenderize a flank steak. A few years ago my friend was in charge of bringing steak for 8 people to a cook out. I was a bit concerned when she arrived with only a very small bag. I predicted a quick trip to the supermarket to supplement her contribution. Out of her bag came these two rolled up, compact, flank steaks, which , incidentally, were the hit of the party and amply served the partygoers. Leftovers are delicious served thinly sliced on a French roll.

1 flank steak, trimmed of fat
1 clove garlic, minced
4 teaspoons soy sauce
2 tablespoons tomato paste
1 tablespoon vegetable oil
1½ teaspoons dried oregano
½ teaspoon pepper, freshly ground

1. Lay flank steak on a large sheet of foil.
2. In a small bowl combine garlic, soy sauce, tomato paste, vegetable oil, oregano and pepper. Spread all over one side of the flank steak and roll the flank steak up jelly-roll style. Wrap in the foil and refrigerate at least 5 hours, or overnight.
3. Grill over hot coals or broil 4 inches from the heat source, turning once, about 4 minutes per side for medium rare. Slice against the grain.
Note: Freeze leftover tomato paste in a small plastic container for later use.

Sunday Pot Roast

Serves 4   Prep   Cooking ⏲ ⏲ ⏲

Pot roast has always been one of my favorites. The meat slices easily when cold, so I make this a day ahead, slice the cold meat and warm it in the gravy, covered, in the oven. Most dishes that have some kind of sauce or gravy are actually enhanced by letting the flavors blend overnight. Serve with noodles or Potato Kugel.

1 beef brisket, about 3 pounds, excess fat removed
1 can (10 ounces) beef broth
1 can (15 ounces) chopped tomatoes
½ cup red wine
3 tablespoons brown sugar
1 large onion, sliced
2 large russet potatoes, peeled and cut into 2 inch cubes
2 large carrots, sliced

1. Place brisket in a Dutch oven and bake, uncovered, in a 400 degree oven for 30 minutes, turning once. This step browns the meat and seals in the juices.
2. Add the beef broth, chopped tomatoes with their liquid, red wine and sugar. Stir to dissolve the sugar. Place the onion around the brisket.
3. Reduce heat to 350 degrees. Cover the brisket and cook for 2 hours. Add potatoes and carrots, cover and cook 30 minutes more, or until the potatoes are tender.
4. Thinly slice the meat against the grain. Serve with potatoes, carrots and pan gravy.

Asparagus Beef

Serves 4   Prep 🕑   Cooking 🕑

This is a quick and easy stir fry to make in the Spring when asparagus is fresh. The cooking time, as with all stir fry dishes, is minimal. Most of the time is spent assembling the ingredients. Use the highest possible heat when stir frying. Broccoli or green beans can be substituted for the asparagus. Serve with steamed rice or Easy Fried Rice.

½ pound flank steak

MARINADE:
1 teaspoon cornstarch
2 tablespoons soy sauce
2 teaspoons sherry or white wine
½ teaspoon sugar

SAUCE MIXTURE:
1 teaspoon cornstarch
½ cup chicken broth

2 tablespoons vegetable oil
1 pound asparagus, washed and cut into 3 inch pieces *
3 tablespoons chicken broth
1 clove garlic, minced
2 slices ginger, each about 1 inch thick, diced *

1. Thinly slice the flank steak across the grain.
2. In a small bowl combine the marinade ingredients - the cornstarch, soy sauce, sherry or white wine and sugar. Place the sliced flank steak in the marinade and toss to coat. Set aside for 15 minutes.
3. Combine the sauce mixture - the cornstarch and chicken broth and set aside.
4. In a wok or a large skillet, heat 1 tablespoon of the vegetable oil. Add the asparagus and stir fry for 1 minute. Add the 3

tablespoons chicken broth, cover and cook over high heat for 2-3 minutes or until crisp cooked. Remove from the pan and set aside.
5. Heat the remaining vegetable oil and stir fry the garlic and ginger for 30 seconds, then add the flank steak and stir fry until cooked through, about 3 minutes. Add the sauce mixture to the wok and stir until the sauce thickens.
6. Return the asparagus to the pan, mix to combine, and serve.
Note: The meat slices easily if partially frozen. Place in the freezer for about an hour and then slice.
* *See How To*

Texas Chili

Serves 6-8   Prep   Cooking ⊕ ⊕

Everyone loves chili and most people claim to make the best. It's great fun to attend chili cook-off contests, see the enthusiasm that chili generates, and taste lots of different versions. Top each serving with grated Cheddar cheese, chopped green onions and a dollop of sour cream or unflavored yogurt. Serve this with either Best Ever Cornbread or warm flour tortillas. Chili freezes well.

3 tablespoons olive oil
1 medium onion, chopped
4 cloves garlic, chopped
1 green bell pepper, chopped
1 pound lean ground beef
1 pound top round steak, fat removed, cut into ½ inch cubes
5 tablespoons chili powder
1 teaspoon dried oregano
1 teaspoon dried thyme
1 can (28 ounces) crushed tomatoes in puree
1 can (15 ounces) peeled tomatoes
1 can (15 ounces) tomato sauce
1 can (12 ounces) beer
1 teaspoon salt
½ teaspoon pepper, freshly ground
1 bay leaf
1 can (15 ounces) kidney beans, rinsed and drained
1 can (15 ounces) pinto beans, rinsed and drained
3 large carrots, peeled, sliced into ¼ inch rounds

Grated Cheddar cheese
Sliced green onions
Sour cream or yogurt

1. In a large saucepan heat the oil over medium heat. Add the onion, garlic and green bell pepper and cook until the vegetables are softened, but not brown, about 4 minutes.

2. Push the vegetables to the side and add the ground beef and the steak cubes. Cook until the meat is browned. Remove all drippings from the pan.

3. Add the chili powder, oregano and thyme, mix well, and cook until the flavors are released, about 30 seconds. Add the crushed tomatoes, peeled tomatoes, tomato sauce, beer, salt, pepper, and bay leaf. Stir to combine, bring to a boil, lower the heat, and cook, covered, for 1 hour.

4. Add the kidney beans, pinto beans and carrots and simmer, uncovered, an additional 30 minutes. Let stand 10 minutes, covered, then remove the bay leaf and serve.

California Steak Burritos

Serves 4   Prep 🕑   Cooking 🕑

Place the meat, warm tortillas, black beans, cheese and veggie relish on the table and let diners make their own burritos.

1 pound flank or skirt steak
Juice of 1 lime
2 tablespoons red wine vinegar
2 tablespoons olive oil
1 clove garlic, minced

1 can (15 ounces) black beans, rinsed and drained
2 cups grated Monterey Jack cheese (½ pound)
8 flour tortillas

VEGGIE RELISH:
½ cup frozen corn, defrosted
¼ cup chopped green bell pepper
1 small carrot, chopped
1 tablespoon diced onion
2 tablespoons red wine vinegar
1 tablespoon lime juice
1 tablespoon olive oil

1. Place the steak in a glass bowl. Combine the lime juice, red wine vinegar, olive oil and garlic and pour over the steak. Refrigerate for 4 hours, turning once.
2. Meanwhile, make the veggie relish. In a small bowl combine the corn, bell pepper, carrot and diced onion. Add the red wine vinegar, lime juice and olive oil, and mix to combine.
3. Warm the beans in a small saucepan. Warm the flour tortillas in the oven, wrapped in aluminum foil.
4. Preheat the broiler. Remove the steak from the marinade and broil 4 inches from the heat, turning once, about 4 minutes per side for medium rare. Let the steak rest for a few minutes, covered with foil, and then slice thinly on the diagonal.

Chicken

I rather like bad wine...one gets so bored with good wine.
Benjamin Disraeli

About Chicken

It makes good sense to take the proper and easy precautions to guard against getting sick from Salmonella bacteria. These bacteria are sometimes found in uncooked eggs, uncooked chicken, as well as in chicken that isn't thoroughly cooked, and the resulting illness, while temporary, is not pleasant at all.

1. Always rinse uncooked chicken in cold water before using.
2. Wash the cutting board and knife in warm soapy water when finished cutting the chicken. Plastic cutting boards can be scoured and are therefore preferable to wood cutting boards.
3. To prevent cross contamination, never use the same unwashed knife or cutting board that touched uncooked chicken to cut or chop other ingredients.
4. Cook chicken thoroughly; the flesh should never be pink. This would be an indication that the chicken isn't completely cooked.
5. Don't eat uncooked eggs or items that have uncooked eggs in them. Some drinks and salad dressings contain uncooked eggs.
6. Don't leave either cooked or uncooked chicken unrefrigerated. After cooking chicken (or turkey), refrigerate leftovers as soon as possible. If taking chicken on a picnic, always place in a cooler with ice.
7. Place frozen chicken in the refrigerator to defrost overnight. If time is an issue, place the frozen chicken in a sealed plastic bag and immerse the bag in a bowl of cold water. Add cold water as needed until chicken is defrosted. This will take about 30 minutes for chicken breasts, longer for legs or a whole chicken.

Roasted Rosemary Chicken and Vegetables

Serves 4   Prep 🕐   Cooking 🕐

This one dish meal is easy to assemble. It looks and tastes as if it came from a very classy Cafe menu. The leftovers are delicious served at room temperature.

1/3 cup olive oil
1/3 cup balsamic vinegar
1 tablespoon dried rosemary
½ teaspoon red pepper flakes
4 chicken breast halves, skinless and boneless, about 1 pound
1 green bell pepper, cut into strips
1 red bell pepper, cut into strips
1 small red onion, quartered
3 carrots, cut into 1 inch slices
1 small eggplant, cut into ½ inch slices

• Preheat oven to 400 degrees
1. In a small bowl combine the olive oil, balsamic vinegar, rosemary and red pepper flakes.
2. Marinate chicken breasts for 5 minutes in olive oil mixture.
3. Place the chicken breasts, reserving the marinade, in a large baking dish.
4. Add vegetables to marinade and toss to coat. Place vegetables in a single layer next to chicken. Pour reserved marinade over the vegetables.
5. Bake for 35 minutes, or until the edges of the vegetables brown. Serve hot or at room temperature.

Sesame Chicken in Pita Bread

Serves 4   Prep 🕐   Cooking 🕐

Pita bread sandwiches are great for a special lunch or a light dinner. Serve with a green salad or Garden Bulgur Salad.

4 chicken breast halves, skinless and boneless, about 1 pound
3 tablespoons lemon juice
½ cup sesame seeds
4 garlic cloves, minced or pressed
1 tablespoon curry powder

2 teaspoons vegetable oil

½ cup unflavored yogurt
2 tablespoons bottled peach chutney
3 green onions, chopped

4 large Pita bread halves
Thinly sliced cucumber

- Preheat the oven to 400 degrees
- Lightly grease a baking sheet with the vegetable oil
1. Pour the lemon juice into a small bowl. Dip both sides of the chicken in the lemon juice.
2. Combine the sesame seeds, garlic, and curry powder. Press both sides of the chicken into the sesame seed mixture.
3. Place on the prepared baking sheet and bake for 20 minutes, or until the chicken is cooked through.
4. Meanwhile, combine the yogurt, chutney and green onions.
5. To serve, place chicken and cucumber slices in the Pita bread and spoon some yogurt dressing around the chicken.

Honey Baked Chicken

Serves 4   Prep 🕐   Cooking 🕑

Serve this moist and flavorful chicken with Easy Fried Rice for a quick and delicious dinner.

4 large chicken breast halves, with skin and rib bones, about 2
   pounds
2 tablespoons honey
2 tablespoons soy sauce
2 tablespoons orange juice
1 tablespoon minced fresh ginger *
3 garlic cloves, minced or pressed
2 tablespoons minced onion
4 green onions, chopped

1. Place chicken in a 9x13 inch pan. In a small bowl combine honey, soy sauce, orange juice, ginger, garlic and onion. Pour over chicken and marinate at room temperature for 1 hour.
2. Preheat oven to 350 degrees. Bake chicken for 40 minutes, or until the chicken is no longer pink.
3. Sprinkle green onions over chicken and cook 5 minutes more.
Note: If you coat the measuring spoon in oil before measuring the honey, the honey won't stick to the spoon.
* See How To

Chicken and Cheese Tostadas

Serves 6   Prep 🕐   Cooking 🕐

Hits the spot when you crave Mexican food.

2 whole chicken breasts, cooked *
2 cups Monterey Jack cheese, shredded (about ½ pound)
6 green onions, sliced
1 can (2 ounces) sliced black olives, drained
¼ cup Salsa Mexican, or purchased salsa
½ teaspoon chili powder

1 tablespoon butter
6 large flour tortillas

Shredded lettuce
Diced tomatoes
1 cup Cheddar cheese, shredded
Sliced avocado or guacamole

• Preheat oven to 325 degrees
1. In a small baking dish combine the chicken, Monterey Jack cheese, green onions, black olives, salsa and chili powder. Cover with foil and bake 15 minutes, or until the chicken is warm and the cheese is melted.
2. Meanwhile, melt ½ teaspoon butter in a large skillet and brown a tortilla until crisp on both sides. Blot on paper towel. Repeat with the remaining butter and tortillas.
3. Remove chicken mixture from the oven and place some on each of the tortillas.
4. Garnish with the shredded lettuce, tomatoes, Cheddar cheese, and avocado or guacamole.
* See How To

Chicken, Cacciatore Style

Serves 4   Prep 🕒   Cooking 🕑

Also known as "Hunter's Chicken", this long time favorite has been updated for an easier preparation and given a '90's twist. This would be good served over pasta, soft polenta or rice.

4 large chicken breast halves, skinless and boneless, about 1 pound
2 tablespoons flour
2 tablespoons olive oil
1 small onion, sliced
3 garlic cloves, crushed
1 green bell pepper, sliced
1 red bell pepper, sliced
½ pound mushrooms, quartered *
1 can (6 ounces) tomato paste
1 cup chicken broth
1 cup red wine
½ teaspoon dried basil
½ teaspoon dried oregano
½ teaspoon dried thyme
½ teaspoon sugar
1 teaspoon salt
½ teaspoon pepper, freshly ground
2 tablespoons capers, drained
1 can (6 ounces) whole black olives, drained

1. Dust the chicken with the flour and shake off the excess. Heat one tablespoon of the olive oil in a large skillet and cook the chicken about 3 minutes on each side, or until the chicken is light brown. Place in a casserole dish.

2. To the same skillet add the remaining olive oil and sauté the onion and garlic until the onion is soft, about 4 minutes. Add the green and red bell pepper and cook another 2 minutes. Push the vegetables to the side of the pan and add the mushrooms. Cook until the mushrooms brown. Pour the vegetables over the chicken in the casserole dish.

3. To the skillet add the tomato paste, chicken broth, red wine, basil, oregano, thyme, sugar, salt and pepper. Stir, scraping up any bits remaining on the bottom of the skillet and bring to a simmer. Pour over the chicken and vegetables.

4. Preheat oven to 350 degrees. Cover the casserole with foil and bake for 25 minutes.

5. Add capers and black olives and bake, uncovered, another 5 minutes.

* See How To

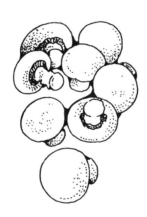

Sweet and Sour Chicken

Serves 4   Prep 🕑   Cooking 🕑

Here's another stir fry dish. The cooking time is minimal. Most of the time is spent assembling the ingredients. Serve this dish with steamed rice.

4 chicken breast halves, skinless and boneless, cut into 1 inch cubes
3 tablespoons soy sauce, divided
1 tablespoon sherry
½ teaspoon salt
4 teaspoons cornstarch, divided
3 tablespoons vegetable oil
1 small onion, cut into 1 inch cubes
2 cloves garlic, thinly sliced
1 large green bell pepper, cut into 1 inch cubes
1 carrot, cut into ¼ inch slices
½ teaspoon red pepper flakes
1 can (8 ounces) pineapple chunks, drained and juice reserved
2 tablespoons red wine vinegar

1. Mix the chicken with 1 tablespoon of the soy sauce, sherry, salt and 2 teaspoons of the cornstarch. Set aside for 15 minutes.
2. In a wok or large skillet heat 1 tablespoon of the oil and briefly stir fry the onion, garlic, bell pepper, carrot, and red pepper flakes for 3 minutes. Remove from the pan.
3. Add the remaining 2 tablespoons oil to the pan. Lift the chicken from the marinade and stir fry the chicken in two batches. Return the first batch of chicken to the pan.
4. Mix the remaining 2 teaspoons cornstarch with the pineapple juice, the remaining 2 tablespoons soy sauce and the vinegar. Pour over the chicken and cook over high heat, stirring until mixture thickens. Add the pineapple and reserved vegetables.

Chicken Curry

Serves 4   Prep 🕐   Cooking 🕐

I love how my kitchen begins to smell when I cook a curry dish. Serve this with lots of steamed rice and pass the pineapple chunks, slivered almonds and diced apple.

4 chicken breast halves, skinless and boneless, about 1 pound
½ teaspoon salt
¼ teaspoon cayenne pepper
3 tablespoons olive oil
1 medium onion, chopped
3 cloves garlic, crushed
1 large green bell pepper, cut in thin strips
2 teaspoons curry powder
1 can (15 ounces) chopped tomatoes
¼ cup currants or raisins
1 teaspoon dried thyme

Pineapple chunks, fresh or canned
Slivered almonds
Diced apple

1. Sprinkle chicken with salt and cayenne. Heat the oil in a large skillet over medium heat and sauté the chicken until brown on both sides, about 7 minutes total time. Remove to a platter.
2. Add onion, garlic and bell pepper to the oil remaining in the skillet and sauté until the vegetables are soft. Add the curry powder and cook 1 minute until the curry is releases its flavor. Add tomatoes and their juice. Stir well.
3. Add the chicken and any juices that may have accumulated back to the skillet. Cover and simmer 15 minutes.
4. Uncover, mix in the raisins or currants and the thyme, and cook until the chicken in no longer pink, about 10 more minutes.
5. Garnish with the pineapple chunks, slivered almonds and diced apple.

Chicken Piccata

Serves 4-6   Prep 🕐   Cooking 🕐

This can also be made with thinly sliced turkey breast; look for "turkey cutlets" in the grocery store.

6 chicken breast halves, skinless and boneless, about 1½ pounds
½ cup flour
½ teaspoon salt
¼ teaspoon pepper
¼ teaspoon paprika
2 tablespoons olive oil
¼ cup sherry, white wine, apple juice or chicken broth
Juice of 1 large lemon
2 lemons, sliced into rounds
2 tablespoons capers, rinsed

1. Pound chicken between sheets of plastic wrap until they are ¼ inch thick.
2. Mix the flour with the salt, pepper and paprika. Pat both sides of the chicken in the flour mixture.
3. Heat oil in a heavy skillet and sauté the chicken until browned on each side, about 7 minutes total time. This might have to be done in two batches. Remove chicken to a platter.
4. Over medium heat add sherry or other liquid to skillet and scrape up the browned bits. Add lemon juice, lemon slices and capers and simmer 4 minutes.
5. Return chicken to skillet, cover, and continue simmering until the chicken is cooked through and no longer pink, about 5 minutes.

Oven Fried Chicken

Serves 4   Prep   Cooking

We stopped eating greasy, fried chicken years ago, and find this a very pleasing alternative. Occasionally I'll have a piece or two of the real thing; no doubt about it, real fried chicken is what the "old days" are all about! Serve this version with Roasted Potato Wedges and Best Ever Cornbread, and feel healthy.

4 skinless, boneless chicken breast halves, about 1 pound
¼ cup unflavored yogurt
½ cup flour, seasoned with salt and pepper
1 egg, beaten with 1 tablespoon water
1 cup dried bread crumbs
¼ cup vegetable oil

- Preheat oven to 350 degrees
- Spread 2 teaspoons of the vegetable oil on a baking sheet
1. Dip both sides of the chicken in the yogurt.
2. Gently press chicken first into the flour, then the beaten egg and finally the bread crumbs. Place on the prepared baking sheet.
3. Brush the breasts with the remainder of the vegetable oil.
4. Bake for 35 minutes, or until the chicken in cooked through and the coating is lightly browned.
Note: Try adding either some grated Parmesan cheese and/or some dried oregano or thyme to the breadcrumbs for a nice variation.

Baked Chicken Rolls with Cheese

Serves 4   Prep 🕐   Cooking 🕐

Treat your guests to something special. Serve with Tomatoes Filled With Corn Pudding and Quinoa Pilaf and be prepared for compliments.

4 chicken breast halves, skinless and boneless, about 1 pound
1 cup dried bread crumbs
½ cup grated Parmesan cheese
1 teaspoon paprika
1½ teaspoons dried basil
4 ounces Muenster, Swiss or Havarti cheese

Flour
1 egg, beaten with 1 tablespoon water
Olive oil, about ¼ cup

- Preheat oven to 350 degrees
- Grease a baking sheet with some of the olive oil
1. Place the chicken breasts between sheets of plastic wrap and pound to about 1/8 inch thickness.
2. Combine bread crumbs, Parmesan cheese, paprika and basil on a paper towel.
3. Cut cheese into 4 long sticks and place 1 cheese stick along the long side of each chicken breast and roll up, completely enclosing the cheese.
4. Dip each chicken roll first in flour, then the beaten egg and finally the bread crumbs. Place on the prepared baking sheet. Brush lightly with the olive oil. Bake for 30 minutes.
Note: A bit of the cheese may escape the chicken rolls. For easy clean up, pour boiling water over that area and gently scrape off.

Spicy Peanut Chicken

Serves 6   Prep 🕐   Cooking 🕐

Try this easy Thai inspired dish with steamed white rice.

4 tablespoons vegetable oil
2/3 cup soy sauce
¼ cup brown sugar, packed
2 tablespoons sherry
1 tablespoon grated ginger *
2 cloves garlic, minced
¾ cup chunky peanut butter
1 cup water
1 teaspoon red pepper flakes
6 chicken breasts, boneless and skinless, about 1½ pounds

1. In a small saucepan combine the oil, soy sauce, brown sugar, sherry, ginger, garlic, peanut butter, water and red pepper flakes. Simmer over low heat, stirring occasionally, for 20 minutes, until the sauce is very thick. Cool to room temperature.
2. Place the chicken in a large baking dish. Pour the sauce over the chicken, turning to coat. Let stand at room temperature for 30 minutes.
3. Preheat oven to 350 degrees. Bake for 20 minutes.
* See How To

Seafood

The lunches of fifty-seven years had caused his chest to slip down to the mezzanine floor. P.G. Wodehouse

About Fish

1. Always buy fish and shellfish in a store or market that does a lot of business.
2. The fish should never smell fishy - ask to smell it before you buy.
3. Refrigerate purchased fish as soon as possible.
4. Use the fish the day you buy it or the next day.
5. Frozen fish is often a good alternative. While not always as tasty, it is fine for dishes that are served with a sauce. Fish that is sold frozen by a reputable company is frozen as soon as it is caught and cleaned, and in that respect is sometimes preferable to fish that has been sold as "fresh" and has perhaps been sitting around for a few days.
6. When buying a whole fish look at the eyes - they should be clear and not glassy.
7. Rinse fish in cold water and pat dry before using.

Sesame Salmon and Spinach

Serves 4   Prep 🕑   Cooking 🕑

Very impressive and delicious, but also so easy to make. The packets can be assembled several hours ahead and refrigerated until dinner time. The individual packets are to be opened at the table. Remind diners to open slowly to allow the steam to escape. There probably isn't a "correct" way to eat foil or parchment wrapped food. I like to cut a slit in the packet and eat directly from this little envelope. Done this way there isn't a mess with collecting and removing the foil. Serve with Rice Pilaf or Easy Fried Rice.

4 salmon fillets, skin removed, about 6 ounces each
1 bunch spinach, washed, stems removed *
4 teaspoons soy sauce
4 teaspoons dry sherry
4 teaspoons Asian sesame oil
4 green onions, chopped

4 sheets aluminum foil, 12 inches x 15 inches

- Preheat oven to 375 degrees
- Place baking sheet in oven to preheat
1. With a tweezer remove all bones from the salmon fillet. Rinse the salmon in cold water and pat dry.
2. Place the aluminum foil sheets on a flat work surface. In the center of each piece place 2 cups of spinach leaves. Top with salmon.
3. Gently crimp the foil around the spinach and salmon to contain the liquid seasonings that will be added. Spoon 1 teaspoon each of soy sauce, sherry and sesame oil, and ¼ of the green onion over each of the salmon fillets.

4. Fold the foil neatly, enclosing the salmon completely. Place the foil packages on the preheated baking sheet. Bake for 12 minutes.

Note: To remove the skin, place the salmon on a cutting board, skin side down, and gently scrape away from the meat with a sharp knife. Or, ask the fishmonger to do it when you buy the salmon.

* *See How To*

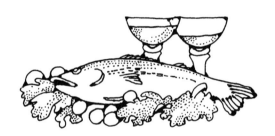

Baked Salmon Steaks

Serves 6   Prep ⏱   Cooking ⏱

Here's an easy, yet elegant, salmon dish. The fish can be assembled up until baking and refrigerated until cooking time. If you do prepare ahead, bring to room temperature 30 minutes before baking. Serve with Rice Pilaf.

6 salmon steaks, about 6 ounces each
1 cup dried bread crumbs
1 teaspoon salt
2 tablespoons butter
1 tablespoon lemon juice
½ cup dry vermouth

• Preheat oven to 375 degrees.
1. Rinse the salmon steaks in cold water and pat dry.
2. Combine the bread crumbs with the salt and coat both sides of the salmon steaks with the crumbs.
3. Melt the butter over medium heat in a large skillet with an ovenproof handle. Brown the steaks on both sides. Remove the skillet from the heat and add the lemon juice and the vermouth.
4. Bake for 15 minutes. Serve with lemon wedges.
Note: If you don't have a skillet with an ovenproof handle, brown the salmon steaks in a skillet then transfer salmon to a casserole dish.

Salmon Teriyaki

Serves 4   Prep 🕐   Cooking 🕐

Often Salmon Teriyaki is grilled; this tasty version is baked. The same marinade can be used if you choose to grill the salmon.

4 salmon steaks, about 6 ounces each

TERIYAKI MARINADE:
½ cup soy sauce
1 tablespoon sugar
2 teaspoons lemon juice
2 teaspoons minced fresh ginger *
2 cloves garlic, minced
2 tablespoons sherry or white wine

1. Rinse the salmon steaks in cold water and pat dry.
2. In a small baking dish combine the soy sauce, sugar, lemon juice, ginger, garlic and sherry. Place the salmon steaks in the baking dish and marinate at room temperature for one hour, turning once.
3. Preheat oven to 400 degrees. Bake for 15 minutes, or until the salmon is cooked through.
* See How To

Baked Trout

Serves 4   Prep   Cooking

What a great way to cook the trout we catch. When the fishing is bad, one can always stop at the grocery store on the way home. No one needs to know.

4 trout, cleaned, heads and tails removed
½ small onion, chopped
1 small carrot, chopped
Salt and pepper
2 teaspoons butter

1 large sheet aluminum foil

- Preheat oven to 375 degrees
1. Wash fish in cold water. Pat dry.
2. Fill the cavities with the onion and carrot and season with salt and pepper. Cut the butter into small bits and place over the vegetables.
3. Place trout on the aluminum foil and carefully wrap to enclose the fish. Bake for 20 minutes.

Shrimp and Corn Stew

Serves 4   Prep   Cooking

This is a thick and hearty soup-stew, perfect for a winter evening. Serve with lots of crusty French bread and a green salad for a quick and delicious dinner.

2 tablespoons olive oil
1 small onion, diced
2 cloves garlic, chopped
1 teaspoon paprika
¼ teaspoon cayenne
1½ cups milk
1 cup chicken broth
1 large russet potato, scrubbed and cubed
1 large carrot, sliced
1 cup frozen corn, defrosted
1 pound raw shrimp, peeled and cleaned *

1. Heat the olive oil in a saucepan over moderate heat. Sauté the onion and garlic until the onion is soft but not brown, about 4 minutes. Add the paprika, cayenne, milk and chicken broth and mix well.
2. Add the potato and the carrot and bring to a boil. Lower the heat and simmer, covered, until the potatoes are just tender, about 20 minutes.
3. Increase the heat to a gentle boil. Add the corn and the shrimp. Cook until the shrimp turn pink and are cooked through, about 3 or 4 minutes.

Note: If using chicken broth from a can, freeze the leftover in a well marked container for use in other recipes. (Don't try to guess what's in the jar a few weeks later.)
* *See How To*

Halibut Alaska

Serves 4   Prep 🕑   Cooking 🕑

I first tasted this delicious dish many years ago on an Alaskan vacation. It has been a family favorite ever since. Despite its easy preparation, it still makes for a nice company dinner. Serve with Roasted Red Potatoes and Green Beans.

4 pieces halibut steak, about 6 ounces each
1 cup dried bread crumbs
¾ cup chopped onion
¾ cup mayonnaise
¾ cup sour cream
Paprika

- Preheat oven to 500 degrees
- Lightly grease a baking dish with butter
1. Rinse the halibut in cold water and pat dry. Spread the bread crumbs on a paper towel. Dip both sides of the halibut in the bread crumbs and then place in the baking dish.
2. In a small bowl combine the onion, mayonnaise and sour cream. Spread over the halibut. Sprinkle with paprika.
3. Bake for 20 minutes.

Red Snapper Veracruz

Serves 4   Prep 🕐   Cooking 🕑

Serve this spicy fish with steamed potatoes.

1½ pounds red snapper fillets
3 tablespoons olive oil
1 large onion, sliced
3 cloves garlic, chopped
1 large green bell pepper, sliced
1 jalapeno pepper, minced *
2 tomatoes, seeded and sliced *
1 bay leaf
½ teaspoon dried oregano
½ teaspoon dried basil
½ teaspoon cumin
1 tablespoon chili powder
¼ teaspoon sugar
½ teaspoon salt
¼ teaspoon pepper, freshly ground

- Preheat oven to 400 degrees
1. Rinse the fish in cold water, pat dry, and place in a baking dish in a single layer.
2. Heat the olive oil over moderate heat in a large skillet. Add the onion and the garlic and sauté until the onion is soft but not brown, about 4 minutes. Add the green bell pepper and the jalapeno pepper and cook 3 more minutes. Add the tomatoes and cook 1 more minute.
3. Add the bay leaf, oregano, basil, cumin, chili powder, sugar, salt and pepper. Cook for 2 minutes. Pour over the fish.
4. Bake, uncovered, for 30 minutes.
* See How To

Scallops with Black Bean Sauce

Serves 4   Prep 🕐   Cooking 🕐

This stir fry is quick, easy and absolutely delicious. Steamed rice would be the usual partner for this dish. One time I was out of rice and served the scallops over whole wheat pasta - what a wonderful taste and color combination this made. Black Bean Sauce with Garlic is available in the Asian section of the supermarket. Be sure to refrigerate the jar after opening.

1 pound bay scallops
1 teaspoon white wine or sherry
1 teaspoon cornstarch
2 tablespoons Black Bean Sauce with Garlic
2 teaspoons soy sauce
1 teaspoon sugar
2 tablespoons water
4 green onions, chopped
¼ pound snow peas, string removed
2 carrots, sliced into ¼ inch rounds
2 tablespoons vegetable oil

1. In a colander rinse scallops in cold water and shake off excess water. Put scallops in a small bowl and mix with the white wine or sherry and the cornstarch.
2. In a small bowl combine the Black Bean Sauce with Garlic, soy sauce, sugar, water and green onions. Set aside.
3. Bring a small pot of water to a boil. Drop the snow peas and carrots in the water and cook for 30 seconds. Drain and pat dry.

4. Heat 1 tablespoon of the oil in either a wok or a large skillet over high heat. Stir fry the snow peas and carrot for 1 minute. Remove from the pan and set aside.

5. Add the remaining oil to the pan and stir fry the scallops with its cornstarch mixture until the scallops turn opaque, about 2 minutes. Add the black bean sauce mixture and continue to cook for 1 more minute, or until the mixture thickens. Add the snow peas and carrots, stir to combine, and serve.

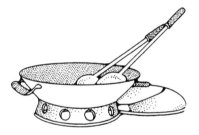

Vegetarian Entrees

When a man talks to you about his mother's cooking, pay no attention, for between the ages of 12 and 21, a boy can eat large quantities of anything and never feel it.
Sarah Tyson Rorer

Lentil Vegetable Casserole

Serves 4-6   Prep   Cooking

This can be a vegetarian entree or a veggie side dish. Even avowed "meat and potatoes" guys like this tasty casserole.

1 cup lentils, rinsed and picked over
4 cups water
2 tablespoons olive oil
1 small onion, chopped
2 cloves garlic, minced
1 medium carrot, cut into ¼ inch rounds
1 stalk celery, thinly sliced
1 medium zucchini, cut into ¼ inch rounds
3 cups spinach leaves, packed *
1 can (15 ounces) chopped tomatoes
1 teaspoon salt
¼ teaspoon pepper, freshly ground
2 tablespoons lemon juice
¼ cup bread crumbs
½ cup wheat germ

1. Place the lentils and the water in a small saucepan. Bring to a boil, reduce heat, and simmer, covered, until the lentils are tender, about 40 minutes. Drain.
2. Meanwhile, heat the olive oil in a large skillet. Sauté the onion and garlic over moderate heat, until the onion is soft but not brown, about 4 minutes. Add the carrot, celery and zucchini and sauté until the vegetables are crisp cooked, about 3 minutes.
3. Preheat the oven to 350 degrees.
4. Add the spinach and tomatoes with their liquid to the skillet and cook 4 more minutes, covered, until the spinach is wilted. Add the salt, pepper, and lemon juice.
5. In a large casserole dish combine the lentils and the contents of the skillet. Top with the bread crumbs and wheat germ.
6. Bake for 25 minutes, or until hot.
* See How To

Italian Vegetable Casserole

Serves 4-6   Prep   Cooking

This is a perfect, make ahead, vegetarian dish. It's fine reheated, and also good served at room temperature.

2 tablespoons olive oil
1 medium eggplant, unpeeled, sliced in ½ inch rounds
1 large potato, peeled and thinly sliced
1 cup dried bread crumbs
1 cup Mozzarella cheese, grated (¼ pound)
1 cup grated Parmesan cheese
2 teaspoons dried basil
1 large green bell pepper, sliced
2 medium zucchini, sliced in rounds
1 can (15 ounces) chopped tomatoes, drained
4 eggs
1 teaspoon salt
¼ teaspoon pepper

- Preheat oven to 400 degrees
1. Pour the olive oil onto a baking sheet and lightly dip both sides of the eggplant in the oil. Spread in a single layer and bake, lightly covered with foil, about 20 minutes.
2. Meanwhile, drop the sliced potato into boiling water and cook over moderate heat until tender, about 6 minutes. Drain and set aside.
3. In a small bowl combine the bread crumbs, Mozzarella and Parmesan cheeses and the basil.

4. Place all the eggplant slices in a 9x13 pan. Sprinkle with ½ cup of the bread crumb mixture. Then make layers of the vegetables followed by the bread crumb mixture. Layer first the potato and ½ cup of the bread crumb mixture, then the bell pepper and ½ cup of the bread crumb mixture and finally the zucchini and ½ cup of the bread-crumb mixture. Lastly, spread the tomatoes over the top and then sprinkle with the remainder of the bread crumb mixture.
5. In a small bowl beat the eggs lightly and add the salt and pepper. Pour over the vegetables and cheeses in the casserole dish.
6. Lower the oven temperature to 375 degrees and bake, uncovered, for 45 minutes.

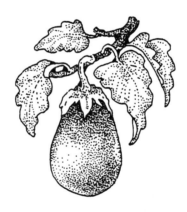

Spinach and Cheese Oven Omelet

Serves 6-8   Prep 🕑   Cooking 🕦

Perfect for brunch or a casual meatless supper. Serve with
Bulgarian Tomato Salad.

2 tablespoons olive oil
1 large onion, chopped
½ pound mushrooms, sliced (2 cups)
1 package (10 ounces) frozen chopped spinach, thawed and well
    drained
8 eggs
1 cup cottage cheese
1 cup unflavored yogurt
1 tablespoon dried oregano
1 teaspoon salt
1/8 teaspoon pepper, freshly ground
1 cup grated Parmesan cheese

- Preheat oven to 325 degrees
1. In a large skillet heat the oil and sauté the onion until tender,
about 4 minutes. Add the mushrooms and continue to cook until
all the moisture from the mushrooms has evaporated and they
have changed color, about 5 minutes. Spread on the bottom of a
10 inch pie plate.
2. Spread spinach over the onion and mushrooms.
3. In a medium bowl beat the eggs. Add the cottage cheese,
yogurt, oregano, salt and pepper, and blend. Pour over the
vegetables in the pie plate.
4. Bake for 35 minutes. Sprinkle with the Parmesan cheese and
bake an additional 5 minutes.
5. Let stand 10 minutes before serving.

Vegetarian Lasagne

Serves 8   Prep 🌑   Cooking 🌑

Serve with warm bread and a green salad. This is a nice alternative to the traditional meat or sausage lasagne.

1 package (8 ounces) lasagne noodles, cooked and drained
2 tablespoons olive oil
½ cup chopped onion
1 large carrot, grated
½ pound mushrooms, sliced (2 cups)
2 cans (15 ounces each) chopped tomatoes, drained
2 packages (10 ounces each) frozen chopped spinach, thawed
    and well drained
1 can (6 ounces) sliced black olives, drained
1½ teaspoons dried oregano
4 cups Monterey Jack cheese, shredded (about 1 pound)
2 cups cottage cheese
½ cup grated Parmesan cheese

- Preheat the oven to 350 degrees
1. Heat the olive oil in a skillet. Slowly sauté the onion and carrot. Increase the heat to high and add the mushrooms. Cook until the mushrooms change color, about 4 minutes. Stir in the chopped tomatoes, spinach, black olives and oregano. Remove from the heat.
2. Place one layer of the lasagne noodles in a 9x13 pan. Cover with ¼ of the Jack cheese, ¼ of the cottage cheese, ¼ of the sauce. Repeat this three more times. Sprinkle the top with the Parmesan cheese.
3. Bake for 30 minutes. Let stand for 10 minutes before serving.

Polenta Vegetable Tart

Serves 3-4   Prep☕   Cooking☕

We love this "Yuppie Pizza". It makes a great lunch or light dinner when served with a green salad and is also a very impressive appetizer.

2 2/3 cups chicken broth
2/3 cups cornmeal
1 cup Provolone cheese, grated (about ¼ pound)
1 cup Pepper Jack cheese, grated (about ¼ pound)
1 roasted red bell pepper (from a 7 ounce jar) cut into
    ½ inch strips
1 jar (4 ounces) marinated artichoke hearts, drained and sliced
1 can (2 ounces) sliced black olives, drained
1 teaspoon dried basil

- Preheat oven to 375 degrees

1. Combine chicken broth and cornmeal in a small saucepan. Bring to a boil, reduce heat to medium, and cook for 10 minutes, stirring frequently, until all the liquid is absorbed and the mixture forms a ball.
2. Spoon the polenta into a 9 inch tart pan with a removable bottom and cool slightly. Place a sheet of waxed paper or plastic wrap over the polenta and use it to press the polenta onto the bottom and sides of the pan.
3. Sprinkle the Provolone and Pepper Jack cheeses over the polenta.
4. Arrange the roasted red bell pepper, artichoke hearts and black olives in an attractive pattern over the polenta. Sprinkle with the basil.
5. Bake for 20 minutes. Cut into slices and serve warm.

Note: Most cooks prefer a coarse ground of cornmeal when making polenta. It is often found near flour in the grocery store, and is called 'polenta'. It can also be found in specialty stores.

Vegetarian Chili

Serves 6   Prep 🕐   Cooking 🕐

Serve this chili with warm flour tortillas and pass the cheddar cheese, unflavored yogurt, green onion and chopped olives. The bulgur gives the impression of ground beef and adds a great texture to this chili.

2 cups tomato juice, divided
1 cup bulgur, uncooked
3 tablespoons olive oil
1 medium onion, chopped
3 cloves garlic, chopped
2 large celery stalks, chopped
1 small green bell pepper, chopped
2 large carrots, cut in ¼ inch rounds
1 jalapeno pepper, diced *
1 tablespoon chili powder
1½ teaspoons cumin
1 teaspoon dried oregano
1 teaspoon salt
1 can (15 ounces) black beans, rinsed and drained
1 can (15 ounces) kidney beans, rinsed and drained
1 can (1 pound 12 ounces) crushed tomatoes in puree
½ cup red wine

Grated Cheddar cheese
Unflavored yogurt
Sliced green onions
Chopped olives

1. Bring 1 cup of the tomato juice to a boil and pour over the bulgur. Let stand 15 minutes.
2. In a large saucepan heat the olive oil over moderate heat. Add the onion and garlic and sauté until the onion is soft but not brown, about 4 minutes. Add the celery, green bell pepper, carrots, and jalapeno pepper. Cook until vegetables begin to soften, about 4 minutes.
3. Add the chili powder, cumin, oregano and salt. Stir well to combine with the vegetables and cook 1 minute. Add the black beans, kidney beans, tomatoes, remaining 1 cup tomato juice, red wine and the bulgur.
4. Bring to a boil, lower the heat and simmer, covered, 30 minutes. If made ahead, add additional tomato juice to thin the chili.
* See How To

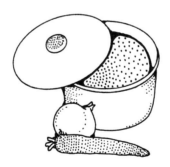

Mexican Crepes

Serves 4-6   Prep 🌀   Cooking 🌀

Serve with guacamole and Salsa Mexicana for a hearty, do ahead dinner. While these crepes are quite filling, hungry folks can eat two, so plan accordingly. Shredded, cooked chicken can be added to the cheese.

6 flour tortillas
2 cups Monterey Jack cheese, grated (about ½ pound)
1 can (4 ounces) diced green chilies
1 can (15 ounces) black beans, rinsed and drained

4 tablespoons butter
4 tablespoons flour
2 cups milk
1 cup sharp Cheddar cheese, grated (about ¼ pound)
1/8 teaspoon pepper, freshly ground

- Preheat oven to 350 degrees
1. Place the tortillas on a flat surface. Spread some of the cheese, chilies and black beans down one side of each tortilla and roll up tightly. Place in a 9x13 pan, seam side down.
2. Melt the butter in a medium saucepan over medium heat. Blend in the flour and cook one minute, stirring constantly. Slowly whisk in the milk and stir until the sauce thickens. Remove from the heat, add the cheese and pepper and stir until the cheese is melted.
3. Pour over the crepes and bake for 30 minutes, or until bubbly.
Note: To prepare ahead, roll the crepes, place in the casserole dish and pour the cheese sauce over them. Refrigerate, then bake as directed.

Vegetable Side Dishes

Cauliflower is nothing but cabbage with a college education.
Mark Twain

Tomatoes Filled with Corn Pudding

Serves 6   Prep 🕙   Cooking 🕙

These make a festive side dish. Shredded cheese can be added to the corn pudding before it is spooned into the tomatoes. Another alternative is to eliminate the tomatoes and bake the corn pudding in a round casserole dish.

6 medium tomatoes
2 eggs, room temperature
2 tablespoons flour
1 tablespoon sugar
¼ teaspoon baking powder
1 cup milk
1½ cups frozen corn, defrosted
1 tablespoon capers, drained
1 tablespoon butter, melted and cooled
½ teaspoon salt
1/8 teaspoon pepper, freshly ground

- Preheat oven to 350 degrees
- Lightly oil a muffin tin
1. Slice the tops off the tomatoes and discard . Scoop out the pulp and the seeds, being careful not to puncture the skin. Invert onto paper towel. Set aside for 15 minutes.
2. Place the tomatoes in the prepared muffin tin.
3. In a medium bowl lightly beat the eggs. Whisk in the flour, sugar and baking powder. Blend in the milk. Stir in the corn, capers, melted butter, salt and pepper.
4. Spoon the corn mixture into the tomatoes. Bake 45 minutes, or until the custard is puffed and lightly browned.

French Potato Casserole

Serves 6   Prep   Cooking ⏲

These tasty potatoes are wonderful with grilled chicken or fish.
They also turn a simple meatloaf into a special dinner.

3 large russet potatoes (2 pounds), peeled and thinly sliced
2 tablespoons butter, cut into small bits
1 cup grated Swiss cheese (about ¼ pound)
1 cup chicken broth
Salt and pepper, freshly ground

- Preheat oven to 425 degrees
- Grease a 9 inch square pan with vegetable spray or butter.
1. Layer one half of the potatoes in the pan, overlapping them. Sprinkle with half of the butter and salt and pepper. Spread the Swiss cheese evenly over the top.
2. Layer the remaining potatoes over the Swiss cheese. Dot with the butter and season with salt and pepper.
3. Pour chicken broth over the potatoes.
4. Bake 1 hour, or until the potatoes are browned on top and the broth has been absorbed.

Potato Latkes

Serves 4-6   Prep 🕐   Cooking 🕐

Latkes are traditionally fried; try this baked version and you will be hooked. Not only are these less greasy, they are also much easier to make. Serve with applesauce or sour cream.

3 large russet potatoes (2 pounds), peeled
1 small onion
2 eggs, slightly beaten
¼ cup flour
1 teaspoon salt
¼ teaspoon pepper, freshly ground
4 teaspoons vegetable oil

• Preheat oven to 425 degrees
• Spread 2 teaspoons of the vegetable oil on each of two baking sheets
1. Grate the potatoes and the onion with either the shredding blade of a food processor or with a hand grater. Don't use a blender; the batter will turn out too uniform in texture as well as too thin.
2. In a medium bowl gently mix the potatoes and the onion with the eggs, flour, salt and pepper.
3. Drop ¼ cup of the batter on the prepared baking sheets and gently press down to form pancakes.
4. Bake for 12 minutes, turn the latkes over, gently press down, and bake another 7 minutes, or until golden.

Potato Kugel

Serves 4-6   Prep 🕐   Cooking 🕐

Also known as potato pudding, this is another favorite from my Russian-Jewish childhood. My grandmother loved to make kugel, and made it for us just as a snack or as part of a special lunch. However, it is really the most wonderful with pot roast and gravy.

3 large russet potatoes (2 pounds), grated
1 small onion, finely chopped
1 small carrot, grated
½ cup flour
2 eggs lightly beaten
¾ teaspoon salt
¼ teaspoon pepper, freshly ground
3 tablespoons vegetable oil

- Preheat oven to 375 degrees
1. Squeeze the moisture out of the potatoes in a kitchen towel. Do this in several batches. Place in a medium bowl. Add the onion and carrot to the bowl.
2. Mix in the flour, eggs, salt and pepper.
3. Place the oil in a 9 inch pie plate. Heat the oil and the pie plate in the oven for 3 minutes, then add the potato mixture.
4. Bake for 45 minutes or until the top of the kugel is golden brown. Cut into wedges.
Note: Since this isn't at its best when reheated, you'll just have to eat it all.

Roasted Potato Wedges

Serves 6   Prep 🕑   Cooking 🕑

Quick and easy, potato wedges make a great side dish, snack or hors d'oeuvre. If served as an hors d'oeuvre, have some sour cream and salsa handy.

2 large russet potatoes, scrubbed and dried
2 large yams, scrubbed and dried
2 tablespoons vegetable oil
½ teaspoon garlic salt
½ teaspoon paprika

- Preheat oven to 425 degrees
- Lightly grease a baking sheet with vegetable spray or oil
1. Cut each potato into six wedges.
2. In a small bowl combine the oil, garlic salt and paprika. Coat the wedges with the oil and place on the baking sheet.
3. Bake for 30 minutes.

Roasted Red Potatoes and Green Beans

Serves 4   Prep 🕐   Cooking 🕐

Easy to make, these veggies are very impressive. Toss leftovers with a vinaigrette for a great potato salad.

3 tablespoons olive oil
1½ pounds small, red-skinned potatoes, scrubbed
½ pound green beans, tips removed
8 large cloves garlic, halved

• Preheat oven to 400 degrees
1. Put the olive oil into a metal baking dish and roll the potatoes around to coat evenly. Cook for 30 minutes.
2. Add the green beans and the garlic, toss to coat with the oil in the pan and cook an additional 20 minutes. The potatoes and green beans will brown slightly.

Mashed Sweet Potatoes

Serves 4   Cooking 🜨

Sweet potatoes and yams seem to be sorely neglected by most potato lovers. Baked, like a russet potato, they are delicious, sweet, supply lots of vitamin A, and are called "velvety" by true fans. Here is a simple, yet more festive preparation. Sweet potatoes have yellow flesh and yams have orange flesh - scratch the skin of the uncooked potato to check.

4 medium sweet potatoes or yams
1 tablespoon butter
¼ cup orange juice
1 tablespoon apricot preserves
½ teaspoon nutmeg

1. Wash potatoes and cut into 2 inch chunks. Place in a steamer over boiling water and cook until tender, about 20 minutes. Alternatively, place in boiling water and cook until tender.
2. Carefully remove the skins and place the potatoes in a medium bowl. Mash with a large spoon, add the butter, orange juice, apricot preserves and nutmeg and mix well.
Note: These potatoes can be prepared ahead and reheated in a 350 degree oven for about 30 minutes.

Easy Fried Rice

Serves 4   Prep   Cooking

This is a great way to use leftover rice. I often make extra white rice so I can make Easy Fried Rice later in the week. This can be prepared ahead and reheated in a 350 degree oven, covered. To make this a main dish meal, add leftover chicken, pork or beef.

2 cups cooked rice, room temperature or cold
2 tablespoons vegetable oil
½ cup onion, chopped
½ cup celery, chopped
½ cup carrot, chopped
½ cup frozen peas
3 green onions, chopped
2 tablespoons soy sauce
½ teaspoon salt

1. In a large skillet or wok heat 1 tablespoon of the oil. Stir fry the onion, celery and carrot until crisp tender, about 2 minutes. Add the peas and the green onion and cook 1 more minute. Remove to a bowl.
2. Heat the remaining 1 tablespoon oil and stir fry the rice, breaking up any lumps. Add the soy sauce and the salt. Add back the contents of the bowl. Mix well.
Note: A non-stick fry pan or wok enables you to use less oil. Also, the clean up is much easier with this kind of cooking surface.

Rice Pilaf

Serves 4   Prep 🕑   Cooking 🕑

Here's a simple, yet elegant, rice dish. It's great served with broiled or grilled chicken.

1 tablespoon butter
½ cup onion, chopped
1 cup rice
2 cups chicken broth
1 cup frozen peas

1. In a medium saucepan melt the butter. Slowly sauté the onion until it is soft, but not brown, about 4 minutes. Add the rice and sauté 1 more minute.
2. Add the broth and bring to a boil. Reduce heat and simmer, covered, until all the liquid is absorbed, about 15 minutes.
3. Remove the pot from the heat and place the frozen peas over the rice. Cover and let sit 4 minutes. Stir the rice with a large fork to incorporate the peas just before serving.
Note: The pilaf can be packed into small custard cups and then unmolded onto the plate for a special presentation.

Quinoa Pilaf

Serves 4   Prep 🕐   Cooking 🕐

Good cooks, as well as natural food enthusiasts, are
rediscovering this grain that was a staple of the Incan diet.
I've seen it on the menus of up-scale restaurants as well as those
considerably more casual. You can buy quinoa (pronounced
"Keen-wa") in a natural foods store.

1 tablespoon butter
½ cup onion, chopped
½ cup mushrooms, chopped
1 cup quinoa
2 cups chicken broth

1. Melt the butter in a medium saucepan. Slowly sauté the
onion until soft, but not brown.
2. Increase the heat, add the mushrooms and sauté until the
mushrooms have browned. Add the quinoa and stir to combine.
3. Add the broth and bring to a boil. Reduce heat and simmer,
covered, until all the liquid is absorbed, about 15 minutes.

Quinoa with Potatoes, Carrots and Corn

Serves 4   Prep 🕐   Cooking 🕐

*Here's another delicious dish using quinoa, a unique protein,
plant-based food. I first came across quinoa on the menu of a
very chic New York restaurant several years ago and introduced
it to my friends, who now love it, too.*

1 tablespoon olive oil
½ cup chopped onion
½ cup chopped celery
2 cloves garlic, minced
¾ cup quinoa, rinsed
2 red potatoes, cut into ½ inch dice
1 small carrot, sliced
1 ¼ cups chicken or vegetable broth
½ teaspoon dried thyme
½ teaspoon dried oregano
½ teaspoon salt
1 cup frozen corn

1. Heat the olive oil in a medium saucepan. Add the onion,
celery and garlic, and sauté until the vegetables are tender, about
4 minutes.
2. Add the quinoa, potatoes and carrot and toss to coat with the
oil. Add the chicken or vegetable broth, thyme, oregano and salt.
Stir to combine.
3. Bring to a boil, lower the heat and simmer, covered for 15
minutes. Remove from the heat, add the corn and mix well, and
let sit, covered for 5 minutes.

Vichy Carrots

Serves 4   Prep 🕑   Cooking 🕑

An easy way to cook not only carrots, but also broccoli and asparagus. I'm a big parsnip fan so I frequently substitute some for half of the carrots. Lots of people ignore the unattractive parsnip because they don't know what it is or what to do with it. It looks like a beige carrot, has a wonderful flavor and is a must for chicken soup. Whenever I buy parsnips, the supermarket checker asks ,"What is this?", and I begin my one-woman ,"you must taste parsnips" crusade. The next time I see that checker he or she assures me that they now like parsnips, too.

4 medium carrots (1 pound), pared and cut into ¼ inch slices
1 tablespoon butter
1 tablespoon sugar
¼ teaspoon salt

1. In a large skillet heat the butter over medium heat. Add the carrots, sugar and salt, and stir to combine.
2. Cover the skillet and cook over medium-low heat for 4 minutes.
3. Remove the cover and cook 2 or 3 more minutes, or until the carrots are tender and all the liquid is cooked off.

Ranch Beans

Serves 8   Prep 🕐   Cooking 🕐

A must for any barbecue! Great with Picnic Flank Steak and Coleslaw, Deli-Style.

2 tablespoons olive oil
1 large onion, chopped
1 can (15 ounces) kidney beans, rinsed and drained
1 can (15 ounces) pinto beans, rinsed and drained
1 can (28 ounces) baked beans
2 cups sharp Cheddar cheese, grated (about ½ pound)
2 tablespoons brown sugar
1/3 cup tomato sauce
2 tablespoons Worcestershire sauce

- Preheat oven to 350 degrees
1. In a large ovenproof casserole heat the oil. Sauté the onion until soft but not brown.
2. Add kidney beans, pinto beans, baked beans, Cheddar cheese, brown sugar, tomato sauce and Worcestershire sauce. Stir to combine.
3. Bake covered for 20 minutes. Remove the cover and bake 15 minutes more.

Fried Tofu

Serves 4   Prep ☺   Cooking ☺

Most people think they don't like tofu. They change their minds when they taste this.

1 pound firm tofu, drained, cut into 1 inch cubes
2 tablespoons vegetable oil
3 cloves garlic, coarsely chopped
4 green onions
1 tablespoon grated ginger *
1 teaspoon sesame oil
1 tablespoon soy sauce

1. In a frying pan heat the oil over moderate heat. Add the tofu and cook until light brown and crisp on all sides, turning frequently. This should take about 7 minutes.
2. Add the garlic and cook another 2 minutes.
3. Add the green onion, grated ginger, sesame oil and soy sauce and cook 1 more minute.
* See How To

Baked Eggplant

Serves 4   Prep 🕐   Cooking 🕐

Eggplant is another of my favorite vegetables. When it is fried, it absorbs lots of oil. This version is baked and therefore less greasy. Try these also as an hors d'oeuvre.

1 large eggplant
4 tablespoons olive oil
½ cup dried bread crumbs
½ teaspoon dried basil
½ teaspoon paprika
½ teaspoon salt
1 egg beaten with 1 tablespoon water

- Preheat oven to 400 degrees
- Brush a baking sheet with 2 tablespoons of the olive oil
1. Cut the eggplant into sticks 4 inches by 1/2 inch.
2. Combine the bread crumbs, basil, paprika and salt on a paper towel.
3. Dip the eggplant sticks in the egg mixture, then roll in the seasoned bread crumbs. Place on the prepared baking sheet.
4. Brush with the remaining 2 tablespoons of the olive oil.
5. Bake for 20 minutes.

Desserts

If this is coffee, then please bring me some tea. But if this is tea, please bring me some coffee. Abraham Lincoln

Grandma's Viennese Chocolate Cherry Cake

Serves 6   Prep   Cooking ●

*This moist and chocolatey cake is one of our family celebration cakes. Serve with a dollop of creme fraiche. ***

3 eggs, separated
10 tablespoons unsalted butter (1 stick + 2 tablespoons)
¾ cup sugar
1¼ cups flour
6 ounces semi-sweet chocolate, melted and cooled slightly
    (chocolate chips are fine)
1 can (15 ounces) tart cherries, drained but not rinsed

• Preheat oven to 350 degrees
1. In the bowl of a mixer place the egg whites. Beat until stiff and they hold their peaks. Using a spatula, scrape into another bowl and set aside.
2. Without washing the bowl or beater, cream the butter with the sugar until soft and light colored. Beat in the egg yolks, then the flour, followed by the melted chocolate.
3. Add the reserved beaten egg whites to the batter and fold in until just incorporated.
4. Turn batter into a 9 inch spring form pan. Place the cherries on the batter in concentric circles. Bake for 1 hour.
5. Cool before removing from pan.
Note: For a special presentation, just before serving place a doily over the top of the cake. Sift powdered sugar over the doily, then carefully remove. A pattern of the powdered sugar will remain on the cake.
* See How To

Banana Yogurt Cake

Serves 8   Prep 🕐   Cooking 🕐

This is a low fat, and yet satisfying, cake. To make it into a fancier dessert, serve with frozen yogurt and sliced fruit.

1½ cups flour
½ cup sugar
1 teaspoon baking soda
2 teaspoons baking powder
½ teaspoon salt
1 large egg
1 teaspoon vanilla
1 cup unflavored yogurt
1 cup mashed ripe banana (1 large)
2 tablespoons vegetable oil

- Preheat oven to 400 degrees
- Grease a 9 inch square baking pan with butter or vegetable spray

1. In a large bowl combine flour, sugar, baking soda, baking powder and salt.
2. In another bowl, beat the egg. Add the vanilla, yogurt, banana and oil and whisk together.
3. Pour wet ingredients over dry ingredients and stir gently until just blended. Do not overmix.
4. Pour the batter into the prepared pan. Bake until the top of the cake is light brown, about 20 minutes.

Gingerbread

Serves 8   Prep 🕐   Cooking 🕐

Here's a light and easy-to-make-version of on old favorite. Serve warm or at room temperature. My friend Laura likes to serve gingerbread with applesauce.

½ cup milk
¼ cup unflavored yogurt
½ cup vegetable oil
¾ cup light molasses
1 egg
2 cups flour
½ teaspoon baking soda
1 teaspoon ground ginger
½ teaspoon cinnamon
½ cup golden raisins

- Preheat oven to 350 degrees
- Lightly grease a 9 inch square pan with butter or vegetable spray

1. In a medium bowl whisk to combine the milk and yogurt. Add the vegetable oil, molasses, and egg. Whisk until blended.
2. In another medium bowl, combine the flour, baking soda ground ginger and cinnamon.
3. Add the flour mixture to the milk mixture. Mix until just combined - the batter will be slightly lumpy. Fold in the raisins. Pour into the greased pan.
4. Bake for 35 minutes. Cool before serving.

Note: Be sure to measure out the vegetable oil before the molasses. If oil is already on the spoon the molasses won't stick.

Blueberry Peach Cake

Serves 8   Prep   Cooking

*Ripe, juicy peaches and fresh blueberries are some of the special
treats of summer. I can't ever get enough. Try this cake slightly
warm. Apples and Italian plums can be substituted for the
peaches and blueberries in the fall.*

½ cup sugar
½ cup unsalted butter (1 stick), room temperature
1 cup flour
1 teaspoon baking powder
1/8 teaspoon salt
2 eggs
3 large peaches, sliced
2 cups blueberries
1 tablespoon lemon juice
1 teaspoon cinnamon

• Preheat oven to 350 degrees
1. Cream the butter with the sugar until light and fluffy. Add the
flour, baking powder and salt. Beat in the eggs. Place in a 9 inch
spring form pan.
2. Cover the batter with the peaches and blueberries, making an
attractive pattern. Sprinkle with the lemon juice and cinnamon.
3. Bake 1 hour.
Note: This is best made in the summer using fresh fruit.

Great-Grandma's Fruit Compote

Serves 6   Prep 🕑   Cooking 🕑

My favorite fruit dessert. It couldn't be easier to make and brings rave reviews. Serve cold or at room temperature, by itself or with poundcake. My Grandmother always said that adding the pits of the fruit added flavor to the syrup.

4 large, ripe peaches or nectarines, or a combination
½ pound cherries
½ cup water

1. Slice the peaches and reserve the pits.
2. Pit the cherries and reserve the pits.
3. Place the peaches, cherries and pits in a saucepan. Add the water. Simmer over very low heat, covered, 20 minutes.
4. Cool, remove the peach and cherry pits. Refrigerate several hours before serving.
Note: A cherry pitter is the perfect tool for pitting the cherries. It can also be used to pit olives.

Apple Pear Crisp

Serves 6   Prep   Cooking

The fresh cranberries add a splash of red and a bit of tartness to this dessert. Buy a bag of cranberries when they come into season and keep them in the freezer until needed. Serve this warm or at room temperature with frozen yogurt or creme fraiche.* It is difficult to find ripe pears at the fruit stand so buy the pears several days ahead and allow time to ripen.

3 large green tart apples, peeled and sliced
3 large ripe pears, peeled and sliced
1½ cups raw cranberries (optional)
Juice of 1 lemon
1/3 cup brown sugar
1/3 cup sugar
½ teaspoon cinnamon
½ teaspoon nutmeg
¼ teaspoon allspice
1/3 cup quick oatmeal
4 tablespoons unsalted butter (½ stick), cut into 8 pieces

• Preheat oven to 350 degrees
1. In a medium bowl toss the apples and pears with the lemon juice. Add the cranberries and place in a 9 inch square pan or pie plate.
2. In the same bowl combine the brown sugar, sugar, cinnamon, nutmeg, allspice and oatmeal. With a pastry blender or your fingertips, cut in the butter until mixture resembles coarse meal. Sprinkle over the fruit.
3. Bake for 40 minutes. Serve warm.
* See How To

Blueberry Peach Crisp

Serves 6   Prep   Cooking

The recipe for this fruit dessert was improvised one summer afternoon. I couldn't have been happier with the results. Certainly other fruit can be substituted - just be sure to have a total of 4 cups of fruit.

THE FRUIT:
2 cups blueberries
6 ripe peaches, sliced
2 tablespoons sugar
1½ tablespoons tapioca, uncooked
2 teaspoons lemon juice

THE TOPPING:
2 almond biscotti
½ cup flour
¼ cup sugar
¼ cup brown sugar
½ teaspoon cinnamon
4 tablespoons butter

• Preheat oven to 400 degrees
1. In a medium bowl combine the blueberries, peaches, sugar, tapioca and lemon juice. Turn into a 9 inch square or round baking dish.
2. Place the biscotti in a plastic bag and crush gently with a rolling pin. The crumbs should be uneven in size.
3. In a small bowl combine the biscotti crumbs, flour, sugar, brown sugar and the cinnamon.

4. Cut the butter into small pieces and work it into the flour mixture with a pastry blender or your fingertips until the mixture begins to hold together. Sprinkle over the fruit.
5. Bake for 30 minutes. Serve warm.

Baked Peaches with Pecans

Serves 4   Prep 🕐   Cooking 🕐

Perfect for mid-summer when peaches are juicy and ripe. Serve with frozen vanilla yogurt and garnish with a mint leaf.

4 ripe peaches
3 tablespoons brown sugar
1 tablespoon butter, cut up
½ cup pecan halves

- Preheat oven to 350 degrees
1. Blanch the peaches to remove the skin.* Halve and pit the peaches.
2. Place the peaches in a casserole dish. Sprinkle with the brown sugar and dot with the butter. Sprinkle with the pecans.
3. Bake for 15-20 minutes, depending on the size of the peach. Serve warm.
Note: Store brown sugar in the freezer after the opening the box - this prevents the sugar from getting hard.
* See How To

Chocolate Chip Oatmeal Cookies

Makes 4 dozen   Prep 🕐   Cooking 🕐

Everyone's favorite cookie. If time is short, make cookie-bars by pouring the batter into a rectangular pan and baking until firm to the touch and the top is brown. Baking time depends, of course, on the size of the pan used. Cut into squares while still warm, and cool in the pan.

1 cup unsalted butter (2 sticks), room temperature
¾ cup brown sugar
¾ cup sugar
2 eggs
1 tablespoon hot water
1½ cups flour
1 teaspoon baking soda
1 teaspoon salt
1 teaspoon vanilla
12 ounces chocolate chips
2 cups quick oatmeal

• Line baking sheets with cooking parchment or aluminum foil, shiny side up
1. Cream the butter with the brown sugar and the sugar until well mixed and there are no lumps.
2. Add eggs, one at a time. Add hot water.
3. Beat in the flour, baking soda and salt. Add the vanilla.
4. Fold in the chocolate chips and the oatmeal. Refrigerate dough at least 2 hours.
5. Preheat oven to 375 degrees. Roll dough into 1 inch size balls and place on the lined baking sheets, leaving room for the cookies to spread. Bake 12 minutes, or until the cookies are light brown.
Note: When baking cookies, place oven racks in the middle of the oven. Reverse the sheets, top to bottom and front to back once during the baking to ensure even cooking.

Chocolate Chip Hazelnut Cookies

Makes 4 dozen   Prep   Cooking 🕐

Chocolate and hazelnuts are a sublime combination. These cookies are the first to disappear from the cookie tray. Hazelnuts are also known as filberts.

1 cup hazelnuts
1 cup (2 sticks) butter, room temperature
¾ cup sugar
¾ cup brown sugar
2 eggs
1 teaspoon vanilla
2¼ cups flour
1 teaspoon baking soda
1 teaspoon salt
12 ounces chocolate chips

- Preheat oven to 350 degrees
- Line baking sheets with cooking parchment or aluminum foil, shiny side up
1. Place the hazelnuts on a baking sheet and toast for 15 minutes. While the nuts are still warm, place them in a kitchen towel and rub vigorously to remove the brown skin. Roughly chop the nuts - don't make the pieces too small. Set aside.
2. Beat the butter with the sugar and brown sugar until fluffy. Beat in the eggs and vanilla.
3. In a small bowl combine the flour, baking soda and salt. Beat into the butter mixture.
4. Stir in the chocolate chips and the chopped hazelnuts.
5. Increase the oven temperature to 375 degrees. Place rounded teaspoons of dough on the lined baking sheets, leaving room for the cookies to spread. Bake for 10-12 minutes, or until lightly brown. Cool on the baking sheet for a few minutes, then remove to a rack.

Peanut Butter Blossoms

Makes 3 dozen   Prep 🕐   Cooking 🕐

What could be better than peanut butter and chocolate? These cookies bring out the child in everyone.

1 1/3 cups flour
1 teaspoon baking soda
1 teaspoon salt
½ cup unsalted butter (1 stick), room temperature
½ cup sugar *plus* ¼ cup sugar
½ cup brown sugar
½ cup smooth peanut butter
1 egg
2 tablespoons milk
1 teaspoon vanilla

1 package chocolate kisses, unwrapped

- Preheat oven to 375 degrees
- Line baking sheets with cooking parchment or aluminum foil, shiny side up
1. Combine flour, baking soda and salt.
2. Cream the butter with the ½ cup sugar and brown sugar. Add the peanut butter, then the egg, milk and vanilla. Add in the flour mixture and mix well.
3. Shape into walnut size balls and roll in the ¼ cup sugar. Place on the prepared baking sheets.
4. Bake for 8 minutes. Remove from oven and press a chocolate kiss in the center of each cookie. Be sure cookie cracks around the edges.
5. Bake another 3-5 minutes.

Raspberry Swirl Brownies

Makes 16   Prep   Cooking

It takes hardly any extra time to make Brownies from scratch, and the difference in taste and texture is remarkable. You can substitute another flavor jam for the raspberry - orange marmalade would be good - or you can eliminate the jam altogether.

4 ounces unsweetened chocolate
½ cup unsalted butter (1 stick)
3 eggs
1½ cups sugar
2 teaspoons vanilla
¾ cup flour
Pinch of salt
½ cup chocolate chips
4 teaspoons raspberry jam

Powdered sugar

- Preheat oven to 350 degrees
- Grease a 9 inch square pan with vegetable spray or butter
1. In a small saucepan melt the chocolate and the butter over low heat. Set aside to cool - the mixture should feel slightly warm to the touch when ready to use.
2. In a medium bowl beat together the eggs and the sugar until the mixture is thickened.
3. Add the vanilla. Slowly beat in the flour and salt, and then the chocolate mixture. Mix in the chocolate chips.
4. Pour batter into the prepared pan. Dot the raspberry jam over the batter. Swirl to incorporate with a fork.
5. Bake for 35 minutes, or until a cake tester comes out clean. Cool on a rack for 2 hours. Sprinkle with powdered sugar and cut into 16 bars.

Raspberry Bars

Makes 2 dozen   Prep 🕐   Cooking 🕐

Thank goodness for bar cookies! These are great to make when time is short and store bought just won't do. Other preserves can be substituted for the raspberry.

¾ cup unsalted butter (1½ sticks), room temperature
1 cup brown sugar
1½ cups flour
1 teaspoon salt
½ teaspoon baking soda
1½ cups quick oatmeal
1 jar (10 ounces) raspberry preserves

• Preheat oven to 400 degrees
1. Beat together the butter and brown sugar until light and fluffy.
2. In a small bowl combine the flour, salt, baking soda and oatmeal. Add to the butter mixture and beat until combined.
3. Spread half of the batter into an ungreased 9x13 pan. Spread with the preserves. Cover with the remaining batter.
4. Bake for 20 minutes or until light brown. Cool, then cut into bars.

Rugelach

Makes 48   Prep 🕐   Cooking 🕐

These buttery treats take some time to make, but are worth the effort. My students claim these are the best they ever tasted. When cutting the dough, think of cutting up a pizza. First cut the dough in half, then each half in thirds, and finally each third into two parts.

1 cup unsalted butter (2 sticks), room temperature
8 ounces cream cheese
2 tablespoons sugar *plus* ½ cup sugar
1 teaspoon vanilla
¼ teaspoon salt
2 cups flour
2 tablespoons cinnamon
¾ cup walnuts or pecans, finely chopped
½ cup currants
1 cup plum preserves

1. In a large bowl beat the butter and cream cheese until smooth. Beat in the 2 tablespoons sugar, vanilla and salt. Slowly beat in flour until well blended. Turn out onto plastic wrap and refrigerate several hours or overnight.
2. In a small bowl mix the remaining sugar with the cinnamon the chopped nuts and the currants.
3. Divide dough into 4 equal balls. On a well floured board roll out one ball into a 12 inch circle. (Keep the rest of the dough refrigerated.) Spread dough with ¼ cup of the preserves. Sprinkle with ¼ cup of the sugar-cinnamon mixture.
4. Preheat oven to 375 degrees.

5. Cut dough circle into 12 equal parts. Starting at the outside edge, roll up to make a crescent. Place crescents on 2 ungreased baking sheets, point-side down. Repeat with remaining dough and filling.

6. Bake for 15 minutes, then reverse the cookie sheets on the oven racks and bake for 10-15 minutes more, or until lightly browned. Cool on wire racks.

Note: Non-stick cookie sheets work well for baking rugelach. If you don't have non-stick sheets, just pour boiling water on any sticky spots when cleaning.

MENUS

A COCKTAIL PARTY

Five Star Artichoke Spinach Dip
Baguette Pizza
Spinach Balls with Yogurt Dip
Hummus and Many Bean Dip with Vegetables and Pita Bread
Teriyaki Cheese Spread
Roasted Garlic
Best Ever Cornbread

SUPERBOWL SUNDAY

Pesto Pizza
Clam and Spinach Dips
Texas Chili
Vegetable Pasta Casserole
Garlic and Onion Bread Strips
Peanut Butter Blossoms
Raspberry Swirl Brownies

SUNDAY BRUNCH

Freshly squeezed orange juice
Great Morning Muffins
Spinach and Cheese Oven Omelet
Bulgarian Tomato Salad
Fresh fruit tray

A ROMANTIC DINNER FOR TWO

Carrot Chutney Soup
Sesame Salmon with Spinach
Quinoa Pilaf
Apple Pear Crisp

THE BOSS COMES TO DINNER

Polenta Vegetable Tart
Tossed Greens with Honey Mustard Vinaigrette
Baked Salmon Steaks
Tomatoes Filled with Corn Pudding
Quinoa Pilaf
Grandma's Viennese Chocolate Cherry Cake

A SPECIAL FAMILY DINNER

Hummus with Pita Bread
Lentil Chard Soup
Middle Eastern Lamb
Roasted Red Potatoes and Green Beans
Baked Peaches with Pecans

A SPRING BUFFET LUNCH

Southwest Chicken Salad
Ginger Rice Salad
Pear Cheddar Salad
New Caesar Salad
Apple Pecan Muffins

THE DINNER PARTY

Shrimp Dip with crackers
Tucson Corn Chowder
Baked Chicken Rolls with Cheese
Rice Pilaf
Blueberry Peach Crisp

From: Mom
Re: Entertaining

The most important thing I can suggest to you is to remember to have a good time, relax and enjoy your guests. People would rather have a meal that isn't necessarily of professional quality, than to spend time with an uptight and distracted host or hostess. Plan ahead, try the recipes before the party, and allow some time to take a walk before your guests arrive.

When my children were small, we were invited to a birthday party for a three year old. The Moms were to enjoy a nice lunch while the kids had theirs. Things seemed a bit tense when we arrived, but I tried to get into the mood of a party. The hostess kept running back and forth to the kitchen, always closing the door behind her. Somewhere along the way it seemed as if I should offer some help. I left the table and started to enter the kitchen when I was stopped by a loud cry of "DON'T GO IN THERE." It was too late because I had already opened the door and could now see why a NO ADMITTANCE sign should have been posted. A cake and some ice cream would have made for a more enjoyable afternoon for sure. But we all learn by our mistakes.

For a sit down dinner, bring out your best tableware. Why save it for your children to inherit? Fresh flowers always add a special feeling to the table. Remember the rule of thumb for centerpieces - the arrangement should be no higher than the height of your fingers if your elbow is placed on the table. It's important for your guests to see each other. (Occasionally this isn't the case!)

Below is a basic table setting for a dinner that would include soup, salad, entree and dessert. The plate above the forks is the bread plate, and the two glasses are for water and wine. Of course, add or subtract any silverware as needed.

Neatly, and quietly (that's the hard part) stack the dishes in the kitchen after each course or quickly place them in the dishwasher. Leave the major clean-up for after your guests depart. We had a friend who would almost whisk the plate from under us to get it washed and put away before the next course. (She also served us chicken livers; my husband thought that a quick removal in that case was fine.)

Keep a journal of who you invited and what you served them. It could be embarrassing to serve the same meal more than once to the same guests.

Finally, be sure to congratulate yourself on a job well done. Start planning your next event. And, don't forget to call your mom.

INDEX

KITCHEN MEASUREMENT CHART

LIQUID AND DRY MEASUREMENTS

a pinch......about 1/8 teaspoon
a dash......a few drops
1 teaspoon......1/3 tablespoon
3 teaspoons......1 tablespoon
4 tablespoons......¼ cup
5 ½ teaspoons......1/3 cup
8 tablespoons......½ cup or 4 ounce
16 tablespoons......1 cup or 8 ounces

LIQUID MEASUREMENTS FOR LARGER QUANTITIES

1 cup......8 ounces or ½ pint
2 cups......1 pint
1 pint......16 ounces
1 quart......2 pints or 32 ounces
1 gallon......4 quarts or 64 ounces

OTHER USEFUL EQUIVALENTS

4 ounces of cheese......1 cup shredded
1 pound of cheese......4 cups shredded
1 stick of butter......8 tablespoons, or ½ cup
4 sticks of butter......2 cups, or 1 pound
1 teaspoon dried herbs......1 tablespoon fresh
1 cup uncooked rice......2 ½ cups cooked
1 cup uncooked macaroni......2 ½ cups cooked
1 cup uncooked noodles......1 cup cooked
8 ounces spaghetti......4 cups cooked
1 large lemon...........4 tablespoons lemon juice

ORDER FORM

Straight Arrow Press
639 Glorietta Blvd.
Lafayette, CA 94549

Please send me _____ copies of
ON YOUR OWN at $14.95 each $_____
Shipping and handling at   2.00 each $_____
California residents add   1.23 sales tax $_____
                              TOTAL $_____

Make check or money order payable to
Straight Arrow Press

Name_____
Address_____
City_____
State_____ Zip_____

Straight Arrow Press
639 Glorietta Blvd.
Lafayette, CA 94549

Please send me _____ copies of
ON YOUR OWN at $14.95 each $_____
Shipping and handling at   2.00 each $_____
California residents add   1.23 sales tax $_____
                              TOTAL $_____

Make check or money order payable to
Straight Arrow Press

Name_____
Address_____
State_____ Zip_____